Kinfolks and Custard Pie

Walter N. Lambert

With original drawings by Hugh Bailey

The University of Tennessee Press

Kinfolks and Custard Pie

RECOLLECTIONS AND RECIPES FROM AN EAST TENNESSEAN

Copyright © 1988 by The University of
Tennessee Press / Knoxville.
All Rights Reserved.
Manufactured in the United States of America.
1st printing, 1988; 2nd printing, 1989; 3rd printing, 1990.

Illustrations: Hugh Bailey
Design: Dariel Mayer
Composition: Tseng Information Systems, Inc.
Printing and Binding: Braun-Brumfield, Inc.

The paper in this book meets the minimum requirements of the
American National Standard for Permanence of Paper for Printed
Library Materials. ∞ The binding materials have been chosen for
strength and durability.

Library of Congress Cataloging in Publication Data
Lambert, Walter N., 1935–
    Kinfolks and custard pie.
    Includes index.
    1. Cookery—Tennessee. 2. Tennessee—
Social life and customs. I. Title.
TX715.L218 1988   641.59768   88-14342
ISBN 0-87049-585-2 (cloth: alk. paper)

This book is dedicated to my wife,
Anne Wayland Lambert.

She has put up with my bad jokes and good food
for twenty-seven years and has thereby
earned many a star for her crown.

Contents

Acknowledgments

I have always looked on acknowledgments as a very risky business. No matter how careful you are, you still fail to remember someone whom it is essential to remember. So many people have helped with this effort that I am sure to forget one of the many. I am grateful to them all.

This effort began when Mollie Biscoe asked if she could interview me for a paper she was preparing for Professor Michael Lofaro of the English Department at UT. She caused me to stop and take a look that led in a fairly straight line to my wanting to set the record down on paper.

I especially appreciate the help I received from my mother and both my Aunt Mary and Aunt Merle. My cousin, Christine Payne, has helped remember many of the details concerning the Weaver family.

Eleanor Boyd Grace has been her usual extraordinary self in helping remember the way things were cooked. She was even more helpful in proofreading and correcting the early drafts. She was joined in these vital tasks by Annarine Hamilton, who read, corrected, and encouraged. These are two great ladies, and I am proud to have them as friends (and proofreaders).

Phila Rawlings Hach brought her enormous energies to this

book as she has to so many things. Typically, when asked to read and comment on the manuscript, she did so. She also provided a four-page description of those things which had worked best for her in marketing cookbooks. She always gives above and beyond.

Alma Lee Walker, who has been my secretary for many years, also graciously read and commented on the manuscript for me. She also put up with me on all those mornings when I had typed late into the night.

Finally, and most importantly, I want to thank my wife Anne. She has typed and retyped and retyped. She has corrected and formatted and helped and pushed. She has questioned and praised and kept me going. She has also let me reveal to the world that Park City is a very long way from Gibbs. Without her help, there would not be a book to read.

To all of these people and dozens more I will be forever grateful.

1

The Place
and the People

We are going to talk about growing up in East Tennessee beginning in 1935. We are going to start in 1935 because that is when I started. This book is to be a fairly narrow account of life in this area during the years when I was growing up. And, it is largely about food. However, as we move along, I believe that you will find, as I have, that it is impossible to talk about the food of a region without talking about the people with whom you shared it and who made it seem important to you. By mingling talk of food and of people, I hope I can give you a glimpse of a particular time and place which has meant enough to me that I think it worth preserving.

In 1935, East Tennessee was rural. It was largely made up of small family-owned farms. Some were subsistence farms, and some were much more—all were changing. Knoxville, though, by 1935 was a thriving community with many of the characteristics of a city. Gay Street, complete with street cars, was a busy, bustling place from the Southern Depot on the north end to the river on the south. Miller's, S. H. George, Hall's and Woodruff's were the places to shop. On Gay Street there were four movie theaters and, for live performances, the historic Lyric Theater, which stood where the Plaza Tower is now located.

Even with all this activity on Gay Street, Market Square was the real center of commerce for those of us who came into Knoxville from the farms which surrounded the city. The east side of the square was the gathering place for a line of trucks from which flowers were sold. The west side (better known as "the spittin' side") was the place for vegetable vendors. Watson's, The Hub Department Store, and, for those of us who were food-obsessed, the Gold Sun Cafe with its piles of fried chicken in the front window were all part of an economy which linked the small farms to the commerce of the city.

The Market House was a center for both commercial grocery operations and individual operators. The commercial operations included fish markets with fish so fresh they were still swimming in tubs (and others, unfortunately, that were less fresh). Meat markets and vegetable shops were also part of the commercial end of the market. By the time I was old enough to remember, a combination of food stalls and fish markets had given the Market House a distinctive smell that was impossible to miss on a cloudy day, even from blocks away.

The folks I knew, however, didn't operate from the stores in the north end of the market but from the small tables in the south end where farm women came to sell extra butter or eggs or other small quantities of farm products. Each tiny, square table had a small square seat attached to one side. It did not matter that the tables were small, because most of these folks didn't have a lot to sell. Yet the small amount of money they made was important to them.

Today, it doesn't seem very far from the center of Knoxville to where I was born—it's only about eighteen miles—but in 1935, that seemed like a long way. Back then, or even as late as 1955,

you didn't have to go far from downtown to be in the country. If you went north through Fountain City toward the area where I was born and lived until I was nine, you would find that Black Oak Ridge made a clear boundary between "America's largest unincorporated city" (I didn't know what they meant then and I still don't know) and farms. Halls Cross Roads was just that—a crossroads with a church, a small school, and the small Avondale Dairy. Only much later did Halls become a suburb.

If you went straight through Halls and on for a few miles, you came to Maynardville. If you were clever, you could find the place to turn off to get to Big Ridge State Park, which was located on the shores of the newly filled Norris Lake behind Norris Dam. But to get to my house—in truth, my grandmother's house—you turned right on Emory Road and went for about three miles. By the time you traveled three miles, there was no question that it was rural. But it was changing.

One important symbol of that change was that an increasing number of families lived on a combination of farm income and income from a job in Knoxville. Many of the men worked at the Knoxville Iron Company, or at one of the many lumber companies, or in the marble quarries. A few of the men and a great many of the women worked in the "cotton" mills "in town."

I don't remember the arrival of TVA power, but I almost remember. I grew up thinking that electricity was useful only to provide a small light and to make the radio work, perhaps because my grandmother believed that it was her personal obligation to pay the Knoxville Utilities Board no more than the minimum amount that was necessary to hook on. She maintained that position for many years—but not, however, without some effort. I still remember her asking me to stop reading and turn off the living room light on a summer night because it would be "cooler with the light off." Many years later when I heard of a building being heated by the return heat from lights, I knew that she may have been right. In the old days, though, I thought that she was simply showing her Scottish ancestry. Whatever her reason, the memory of sitting in the dark in that living room (or even sitting on the front porch with the door and windows open) and listening to *The Lone Ranger* or *Amos 'n' Andy* still seems wonderful. All these things come back to me as somehow particularly representative of the East Tennessee of the 1930s and 1940s, a time of transition.

In the 1930s and 1940s, this area was by no means isolated. The days were gone when people felt crowded if they could see smoke from their neighbor's chimney. What was not gone was a sense of community which still made people feel responsible for those who happened to live nearby. Although this sense of community shouldn't be taken to mean that you liked folks just because they happened to live next door, it did mean that you knew them and shared with them. You shared spare time, and you shared work.

From those days I remember clearly the threshing crews which were made up of all the men in the community, moving from farm to farm with the threshing machine to take care of the small plots of wheat that each farm had. While threshing was hard work, it also had an element of a social event which certainly made the work easier. It now seems much funnier than it did then to remember asking a small child's terribly serious question about what was wrong with a baler used with the thresher and being told that the baler had a brier in its finger.

People got together to thresh wheat, to make molasses, to kill hogs, to tell stories, to assist at a birth, to celebrate a wedding, to worship God, and to bury the dead. In all these events, a central element was a concern for the people who made up your community, and *the* central element was food. The wake, wedding, church supper, or threshing crew all made food necessary. But food was more than that: it provided a straightforward way of saying that an event was important and that you cared for the people who were taking part in it.

As I've told you, this book is about both food and people.

Because I want not only to talk about the food we ate but also to help you know how to prepare it for yourself, I'll mix the recollections with recipes. Both are important to the book, for together they show a style of life which is very close at hand yet now seems to be fast disappearing. Over the years I have developed a taste for fine food, and I have married someone with similar tastes. I have eaten at some of the finest restaurants in some of the most cosmopolitan cities in America and abroad. I have studied the mysteries of the five schools of Chinese cooking, and if forced to choose only one cuisine for the rest of my life (God forbid), I would probably choose Chinese. But I still remember the taste of that custard pie that my grandmother had hidden in the pantry just for me on a Sunday long ago—a pie that all the visiting relatives would have eaten every bite of, had they known it was there. I am not sure how much of that memory is sweet because of the pie and how much of it is because of my grandmother. I know, however, that I believe the way we felt about food then (and some of us still feel) is important and that I want to write it down.

I know that when a neighbor was sick, you could always show that you cared by packing some food in a basket and walking across the field with it. I know that when a family experienced a death, you could show that you wished to make their life simpler

by taking them food. I know that in either of these cases, you could just tell the people that you cared, but I also know that a gift of food went beyond mere words. What I want to recapture by sharing these stories and recipes with you is that sense of community we got from sharing food that wasn't a necessity but represented neighbors taking their time and limited resources to show how they felt.

What I want to share with you isn't scholarly research. I haven't studied all the folkways that pertain to food in Tennessee. I haven't made a list of all the ingredients or done a survey to determine the most commonly served dishes or even the most usual means of preparation. I include details because I remember them as important. I include recipes because I think they are good or because other people I knew thought they were.

Neither is this book comprehensive. I have talked to my mother and my aunts. I have talked to friends who have the reputation of being good traditional cooks. I have remembered stories and recipes that my grandmothers told me. Through the years I have even written down some recipes. With all of this, hundreds of recipes and thousands of variations are possible. I am sure that you know many of them. Perhaps I'll inspire you to preserve some of them by writing them down, whether you make a book from them or not.

Some of these recipes I use regularly. Others I have done from memory and have retested to see if I could still do them. In most cases, I have had to arrive at amounts of ingredients for the recipes almost by trial and error. If either of my grandmothers had a measuring cup or measuring spoons, I never saw them. They cooked by feel and by the kind of knowledge that's acquired only through some sort of generational osmosis. My mother cooks today in much the same way. The amount to put into the pot is determined by some hidden source of the rightness of things and the number of people who happen to be coming for dinner (if you happen to know!). I have attempted to reduce all that to measurable proportions.

I have also attempted to impose some structure on these memories, but the structure is arbitrary and artificial at best. It is designed mostly for my benefit and may be a positive hindrance for you if your only intent is to find a recipe like grandmother used to make (I've tried to make amends by including a relatively coherent index). If, as some people do, you simply intend to read from front to back, then the plan I have imposed will make a little more sense.

Like the life of an East Tennessee farmer in the 1930s or 1940s, this book is arranged around the changing of the seasons. I have started in the spring because I like the spring. I hope you'll indulge my arranging things around a few events, but that's how life seemed back then. I like all-day dinners with singing on the grounds (you do it your way and I'll do it mine, but I do remember the food as much better than the singing on those hot summer days). I even like wakes (with the body in the parlor) while everyone sits on the front porch and eats and tells stories, fondly remembering the person, not the body. Because I like these memories and because I believe they are important to what life was like here, I have included them.

Unfortunately, this plan doesn't allow putting all the meats together and all the vegetables together and all those other neat arrangements that you might expect from a regular cookbook. In fact, those systems are probably more artificial than the plan I'm using, but they are more familiar. And so again I beg your indulgence. Use the index because, as Mrs. Peters taught me in the sixth grade, it's good for you to do things for yourself.

Now, before we get into the body of these recollections and recipes, which I hope will bring those times to life for you, I think it will help you to know a little more about me and why I feel the way I do about food.

I was born at my grandmother's house on Emory Road between Halls and Harbison's Crossroads in the fall of 1935. My mother and father were next-door neighbors. When they married, they moved in with his mother and stepfather and lived there until I was seven. The two families filled four houses scattered about a half mile along a country road. In both families, there were untold scores of relatives who lived nearby or in the city and came regularly to visit. Between my two parents, the extended family reached enormous proportions.

Until I was seven, I was the only child in these four houses on a regular basis. I had a great many cousins, some older and some younger, but they lived somewhere else and just came to visit. I lived there. I could walk from house to house, shopping for the best deal. I hope life was as good as I remember it, because

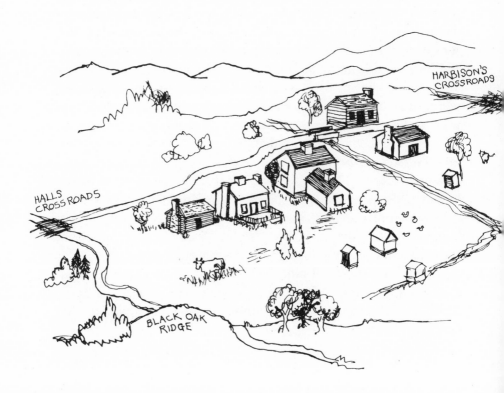

I remember it as something really special. And in the center of those memories are big family meals. And in the center of those memories of the meals are the memories of the people who were connected with them.

Some people will be particularly important in the course of telling you about those times. I will try to tell you enough about the people to help you understand what is happening. To my paternal grandmother, Mammy Dossett, or to my maternal great-grandparents, Grandpa and Granny Weaver, or their daughter, my grandmother, whom I called Ma Freeman in the years I was growing up, having good food was always important. My mother and father learned it from them, and they have passed an appreciation of food on to me and their other children. We never had money, but my mother still says with some pride: "Nobody ever left my house hungry." She meant it then, and she means it now.

My two grandmothers will sometimes seem to dominate my memories. It's not that other people were not as important but just that both of my grandmothers were the sort of women who naturally dominated things. My Mammy Dossett, with whom we lived, was one of six children—a middle child in a family made up of five daughters and one son. That son, my uncle Walter (whose namesake I may be, though there is some disagreement about that in the family) remained very important to my grandmother. He and his wife were regulars in the strange household that I lived in; they came to be fed and be given milk, butter, and eggs. Mammy's sisters, Tennie, Telia, and May, with their families, were also regulars, but somehow Mammy Dossett always believed that Uncle Walter was special and that whatever he wanted he should have. She always seemed to feel the same way about me. Maybe it was the name.

While I'm on names, I should also mention forms of address. In the families I knew, the most common form of address for a grandmother was either "Mammy" or "Granny." I knew only one "Big Mama." Grandfathers were called "Grandpa" or "Dad." I knew one "Big Daddy" (you will be comforted to know that he was married to "Big Mama"). It was not uncommon to use the full name, saying "Mammy Dossett" rather than just "Mammy." Aunts and uncles were called "Aunt" or "Uncle." "Sir" and "Ma'am" were expected, and forgetting them could bring a sharp rap on the side of the head. It was perfectly acceptable not to use a child's name, but simply to say "Boy" or "Girl." Children were around to be handy. Adults were around to be respected.

Mammy had married my grandfather, who was much older than she was, when she was very young. They quickly had six children. One child died soon after he was born. When my father was about twelve, he had polio (called inflammatory rheumatism by a country doctor) and was left permanently crippled. When the youngest of their children was four or five, my grandfather died. Some years after his death, my grandmother married a man who had three children about the ages of her three youngest and she treated them exactly as she did her own.

When we lived at her house, I thought she was very, very old. (In fact, she was almost exactly the same age I am now.) She had lived a lot and had taken a lot in stride, but she was no saint. She was clearly accustomed to having her way and knew how to keep on having it. I am told that all of life is about control and compromise. Mammy knew a lot more about control than about compromise. If speaking softly worked, she spoke softly. If threatening was needed, then she threatened. If crying worked, she cried. If it was absolutely necessary, she fainted. I thought the universe revolved around her.

My other grandmother was also a middle child in a large family. She had my mother when she was young and was then left to bring her up alone. This she did by working in the city or anyplace else she could find work while my mother lived with a lot of other people at her grandmother and grandfather's. As I grew up, Ma Freeman was always the person who had been places and knew about things. Although she was the person who came to visit on weekends and sent packages in the mail, her presence was as strong as if she had been right next door. In fact, her parents did live next door.

Granny and Grandpa Weaver had scratched out a living for their six children on the little farm where they lived. Later in life, they supplemented their meager earnings with a second small farm about a mile away. I believe that one of their daughters had bought this second farm and allowed them to use it—I seem to remember some dispute about it after Grandpa's death. Disputes, of course, were the standard means of operation. Neither family was given to quiet, logical discussions.

From their two small parcels of land, the Weavers grew food for their own use and enough to sell to buy the few additional items they needed. My Grandpa Weaver was the only person I knew in their community who grew cotton. Granny liked to have her own cotton to put into quilts. She picked the cotton, seeded it by hand, and carded it into neat little rectangles with cards which her mother had given her. In case you don't know, a cotton card looks like a small paddle with thin spikes set close together on one side. The cotton was drawn across these spikes to pull the fibers into roughly the same direction and make a uniform shape about a half inch thick. Carding cotton was ideal work to do by fireside on a winter evening.

Grandpa also grew wheat, corn, and tobacco to sell, just as almost everyone else did. Some of the wheat and corn, however, he had ground for his own use, a dying practice by the time I came along. By then, most people grew corn to sell or to feed the animals and bought their cornmeal. But Grandpa Weaver didn't trust any cornmeal he hadn't seen ground. He even had his own wheat ground to make sure he had good whole wheat flour.

Together, the Weavers, Mammy Dossett, and Ma Freeman exercised a role in my early life that seems strange today as the extended family has shrunk. Perhaps my start in school will illustrate the true dominance my extended family exercised in my life. When it became time for me to go to school, I announced that I didn't intend to go. Mammy Dossett's pronouncement was that she did not believe I would learn anything if I was made to go and, therefore, should be allowed to wait until the next year. I waited.

When the next year came, I still wasn't crazy about the idea of going to school. However, cooler heads (my mother and father) prevailed, and I was sent to Gibbs School and entrusted to the kind hands of Mrs. Neva Cardwell. "Miss Neva" was not exactly a new teacher—in fact, she'd taught my mother in the first grade. About the third day, I decided that I had learned all there possibly was to know, so I left the classroom and started down the long hall that led out of the school.

Just then, who should be coming up the hall but Mr. H. G. Loy, the principal of the school. As was often the case in small, rural schools, "Professor Loy" knew me and my family. "Where are you going, son?" he asked pleasantly. "I'm going home," I announced. Still in a pleasant voice, he suggested that I reconsider and return to the classroom. In a less than pleasant voice, I informed him that I had no intention of doing so.

Whereupon, he reached out with one of his big hands, took me firmly by the shoulder, and turned me around toward the classroom. With the other he swatted me firmly on the backside and said, "Boy, go back in that classroom and do what Miss Cardwell tells you." Having had the situation explained to me so succinctly, I went back into the class, did what I was told, and have had my feet firmly set on the road to knowledge ever since.

My recollections have to do with things that are peculiar to the country living of that time. This can be seen in my own family. I married Anne Wayland, who was raised in the Park City section of Knoxville. Her father, Charles F. Wayland, Sr., traveled throughout East Tennessee for a wholesale dry goods company for many years, and people still tell me about remembering his calling on their parents. Although it was clear that he always felt tied to the countryside, his family always lived in the city, and the life I am describing had little resemblance to the way they lived. Much of what I will be telling you about is as strange to my wife as it may be to you, even though we grew up about the same time and only about twenty miles apart.

I learned to cook as a child and have always enjoyed it. It might not have fit with the customs of the times for a boy to learn to cook, but necessity can be a powerful teacher. You see, I am the oldest of eight children. I was seven when my next brother was born. Soon after his birth, we moved from my grandmother's to a farm on Washington Pike near Corryton, Tennessee. With a lot of children, a farm to help take care of, and my father working in the city, my mother needed all the help she could get. So in order to help, I learned to cook.

I believe that my earliest memories of cooking are when I was about nine or ten. My mother was ill and told me that I would have to help. I peeled potatoes and prepared other vegetables, taking them to her bedside to see if I was doing it properly. I continued to help even when she became better. It was understood that I would help with the kitchen chores as much as with any other chores which were to be done. If I were completely honest, I might admit that I enjoyed this a lot more than I enjoyed hoeing the garden, and it is possible that my help with the cooking became a way to avoid some of the more unpleasant tasks on the farm. (I see no real reason, however, to be quite that honest.)

It is that sense of a particular time and special place that I hope you will feel with me. For several years, I have talked about the book I was trying to write to anyone who would sit still for a few moments and listen—I have attempted to recapture some of that spontaneity on these pages. For those of you who may be more interested in the reminiscences, I hope the recipes do not get in the way. For those of you who want only the recipes, bear with me and we will get to them. Perhaps many of you will have grown up as I have in a world where remembering and eating always seem to be intertwined.

My fondest hope is that I will be able to share some of my feelings about food and be able to introduce you to some of the people who have meant the most to me. Further, I am convinced that we must save the recipes which were part of that time. Today we have new and sometimes even better ways of doing things. Fine! Learn them and use them. But that doesn't mean that we should lose sight of the way things used to be done—and we shouldn't let the next generation forget that we have truly come a long way in the last fifty years. Perhaps what we all need to remember (or, in some cases, learn for the first time) is that in proper proportion, nothing is better than hard work, kinfolks, and custard pie.

2
Spring

Everyone has some way of knowing when winter is over. I have asked many people who grew up in East Tennessee how they first knew it was spring. They talked about robins and crocuses and many other things. For many people, though, the surest sign of spring in the old days was the taste of wild onions in the milk. If you don't understand what this means, it's a sign of how much times have changed. But if you're over fifty or grew up on a farm, you know that cows lived partly on feed but also partly on open pasture. In early spring, wild onions grew abundantly in the pasture and cows loved them. (While the onion taste wasn't too bad in cottage cheese, it really made chocolate cake taste funny.)

For me, however, as nice as robins and crocuses are and as clearly as the taste of wild onions comes back, spring really begins with the first fresh vegetables. The hardy (and really brave, since weather has never been particularly predictable in East Tennessee) believed that the earliest crops should be planted on February 14 if the ground was not frozen and the signs were right. These crops would certainly include English peas, onions, and leaf lettuce if you had a cold frame or some other way to shelter the vegetables against bad weather.

Both peas and onions were really safe to plant even this early because they wouldn't sprout until it was warm enough anyway. Later, and certainly by mid-March, you would go ahead with leaf lettuce and onion sets for green onions. Other spring vegetables would come later, with corn and beans planted on Good Friday.

While I don't know enough (or care enough) to talk about gardening, I do know it is impossible to look at food customs of the 1930s and 1940s without recognizing that much of what was available to eat depended upon one's ability to raise it. Furthermore, the taste of food is greatly influenced by its freshness and the way it is grown. Therefore, when I digress from time to time to talk about planting and whether the frost will spoil the rhubarb, it is just because if you didn't grow it, you probably didn't eat it.

No account of growing vegetables in East Tennessee would

be complete without at least a mention of planting "by the signs." Country people believed then—and many still do today—that different crops should be planted at different times in the monthly astrological cycle. Most of the people I knew followed the signs not by their astrological names but by the corresponding body parts which were associated with them.

For example, Aries is the head, Taurus is the neck, Gemini (the Twins) is the arms, Pisces is the feet, and Leo is the heart. In all of these, there are certain associated characteristics with regard to planting. The head and neck are considered to be only fair signs for planting except for plants you want to grow tall. Virgo, the bowels, is a very bad sign for planting any fruits and vegetables; plants started in this sign produce blooms and no fruit.

One of the strangest of these customs has to do with Leo. Logic would say that this should be a good sign, since the heart is often used as the sign of love and all that is good. But, in fact,

just the opposite is true. The heart has traditionally been viewed as the worst time to plant. Instead, it is looked on as a good time to kill weeds or bugs.

It might be wise to note that like religion, belief in this system could have considerable variation. I simply know that because generations of my family have told me, that it is fair to plant in the head, good to plant in the arms or legs, and that cucumbers should be planted in the "twin signs" of May.

This planting system made the almanac an essential part of any well-equipped household. Without it, you could not be sure of exactly where you were in the cycle of the moon or the positions of the constellations. I don't remember, much less follow those signs today, but I still never fail to note where I am when I see the new moon for the first time each month. That determines how your month will be, you know. If you happen to be going up hill when you see the new moon, you are in for a good month. If you are on level ground, things will continue about the same. However, if you happen to be going down a steep hill, watch out! I assume the moral of this story is keep your eye on the ground if you are going down a steep hill.

Another sure sign of spring was going out to look for "dry land creases." This particular type of wild green, which I have subsequently identified as winter cress, grew in fields that had been cultivated the year before. The greens grew in a flat circle very low to the ground, and you wandered through the previous year's cornfield looking for the green leaves of **creases** among the brown of the field. They were cut off at the top of the ground with a knife. After being washed thoroughly, they were parboiled, drained, and cooked again in a small amount of salt bacon grease until any excess water had cooked out. Creases were a wonderful start to spring. I haven't tasted them in years, but I still remember their sharp flavor.

I have been told that some people tend to improve things as they remember them from some distance in time. Some people might even assume that's happening in what I'm doing now. The following example will prove beyond a shadow of a doubt that I am not. The stream below our springhouse was filled with watercress, but we didn't eat it.

We didn't even have the excuse of not knowing it was edible, since Aunt Margaret, who came to visit every Sunday (well, almost every Sunday) with her husband, Uncle Walter, liked it. Of course, that may have been the reason it didn't appeal to the rest of us. Aunt Margaret was a great, fat, loud-talking woman who had been raised in the city. She was regarded as something less than perfect by her sister-in-law, my grandmother. My grandmother and her three other sisters whispered that Margaret even expected their only brother to help keep the house clean. Not only that, Aunt Margaret would eat *anything,* and so her assurances that those shiny green leaves were delicious were simply not recommendation enough. Although I didn't learn to appreciate watercress until later, I'm afraid that grocers must bear my everlasting scorn when they charge thirty-nine cents for a scraggly bunch of cress which is not half so nice as what I could have gotten just by walking down to the spring branch.

Even though I promise that this will not be *Foxfire Twenty-Four*, a word about the springhouse might be in order. I remember clearly when we bought our first refrigerator, an enormous four-doored contraption that made a lot of noise and was, therefore, relegated to the back porch, where it would not disturb anyone. In case you are curious, we never had a washing machine on the front porch. Every civilized person knows that front porches are to sit on and rock and not to show off your appliances—only our far less sophisticated cousins who lived much further back in the country (sometimes as far back as two or three miles) didn't understand that difference. The refrigerator replaced an icebox we had used for some years to supplement the springhouse that had previously been our only way of keeping foods cool. That icebox, by the way, was stocked by a truck that came a couple of times a week from an ice company in Knoxville. One of my jobs as a child was to hang out the sign saying how much ice we would need that day.

The springhouse was an ingenious device which consisted of a box placed in a stream bed just below the point where a freshwater spring flowed out of the ground. Since this water came out of the ground at a temperature much cooler than the air, it kept cool whatever was set into the water. Sometimes this box was only a simple log frame, sometimes a fairly fancy, concrete structure. A shelter was then built over the whole thing, and you had instant cooling for milk, butter, and anything else that needed it. The water flowed into the box at the upper end and out at the bottom. A separate, smaller box could be immersed in the water or a shelf could be built just above the water level to keep food cool that you did not want to get wet. That's all there was to it. Because many people had large quantities of milk on hand, they often continued to use these springhouses long after they had other kinds of cooling. (The remains of springhouses can still be seen throughout our area.)

At Mammy Dossett's the springhouse was some distance away, across the pasture field, and at my mother's family home it was even further away, in a stream which flowed through past their house. In each case, a well with a hand pump installed had been dug very near the back porch of the house. Because the Weavers had even more milk than most people (they sold both milk and cream), they had built a milk house very near the back of their dwelling and regularly pumped fresh water from the well to flow through the box containing the milk to keep it cool. While the pumping was not that easy, it was easier than walking back and forth to the old springhouse, and there were always somebody's children around who could do the pumping. (Water in the house came much later.)

Besides "creases," my family ate only one other kind of wild greens, and it also grew in the spring. We thought that pokeweed (or poke greens or poke salat) was the ultimate spring tonic. The plant is still easy to find, even in the city. If you should happen to be so culturally deprived as not to be able to recognize its broad, shiny green leaves and slightly reddish stem, I would recommend that you look it up in one of the many good books around on wild greens and next April go looking for it. If you live in a well-kept suburb where every roadside is curbed and guttered and every back yard is kept smooth as carpet, you must drive out along a less well-kept country road somewhere. Fortunately my neighbors are not that compulsive, and I can find this delightful spring green in the privacy of my own neighborhood.

A word of caution is necessary about poke. It must be picked when it is very young. People have their own rules about how big is too big. Some say the stem should be no bigger than your little finger. Others will tell you that the plant should have no more than six leaves. Others still will talk about the size of the leaves. Whichever guideline you use, it is important to pick only small

plants. Calling poke a spring tonic is simply a polite way to say that even when picked small, it has a mild laxative effect. Allowed to grow larger, it becomes downright poison and should not be eaten. Remember, never pick poke that is more than 8 inches tall and always parboil it and discard the parboiling water.

If you are lucky enough to identify it and find it to pick, cooking **pokeweed** is very easy. Just wash the greens carefully a couple of times and pick through them to be sure you haven't included dead leaves or other debris. Put them in a large pot and cover generously with cold water. Bring them to a boil and boil for about fifteen minutes until they begin to get tender. Drain the greens thoroughly and then fry them in the fat from a couple of pieces of salt bacon until all excess moisture is cooked out. Be sure to stir them occasionally. When the greens get fairly dry, stir in a couple of well-beaten eggs and allow them to cook while you are stirring constantly. When the eggs are well set, you are ready to eat. If you are concerned about what to serve with what, I suggest poke greens, hot cornbread, and cold milk as the perfect combination. If you have fried some salt pork just to get the grease to cook the greens in, this meat makes the only possible addition.

Sometime later we will talk about the role of pork in the diet during the period when I was growing up. Right now it should be sufficient to say that when rural East Tennesseeans in the era when I was growing up said "meat," they, like the Chinese, meant pork. Only two things were used for seasoning vegetables, butter and pork fat. Excess pork fat was saved to be used for seasoning. Beans (either green or dried) were cooked with salt-cured fat pork. If you fried something in fat, you used lard or butter. Pastry was made with lard or butter. You used it because it was all you had.

I've been talking a good deal about wild greens. We also ate domestic greens. Usually turnips—both for turnips and for greens —mustard, kale, and sometimes collards were planted in the fall and were a regular part of the diet. If they were available in the spring, and they often were, it was because they "wintered over," and those greens you planted in the fall sprouted and grew again in the spring. In "Fall" we will talk a good deal more about this important food.

One of the vegetables that I most associate with the coming of spring is English peas. They were planted very early because they were resistant to late frosts, if not late freezes. Picking and shelling peas could be a family project carried out in the early evening so as to have them ready for dinner the next day. Fresh peas are wonderfully tender and need little except butter to be delicious. Fortunately, they are often available in grocery stores and farmers' markets. I recommend cooking them in any of the following ways for a real treat.

Green Peas

Shell and pick over about two pounds of English peas of any of the varieties except those green marbles that are used for commercial freezing. Place the peas in a heavy kettle with a tightly fitting lid with about ½ cup of water. Cover and bring slowly to a boil. Cook about fifteen minutes or until the peas just begin to break up. Remove the cover and add about two tablespoons of butter and cook uncovered until the butter melts. Add salt to taste and serve immediately.

Variations.

(1) Cook peas exactly as above except use fresh whole milk instead of the water and reduce the butter by half.

(2) Prepare peas exactly as above except place them in a pot which has been lined with freshly washed and still wet leaf lettuce. Add no water. Cover with additional lettuce leaves. Cover the pot tightly and bring very slowly just to boiling. Hold just at boiling and cook until tender. Remove the peas to a bowl and add butter and salt to taste. Discard the lettuce; it has served its purpose.

Because we often served them together and because their tastes are so complementary, I always think of homemade **cottage cheese** with spring peas. In this era of pasteurized, homogenized milk, making cottage cheese at home is not so easy as it once was. If you can find milk which has been pasteurized but not homogenized, it is easier. Homemade cottage cheese can also be made with non-fat dried milk, but it is not so good. I grew up with cottage cheese made from excess skim milk. The process is extremely simple, so if you can find the proper kind of milk, you may want to give it a try. First, skim milk was allowed to sour and fully clabber. The clabber was then poured into a cheesecloth and hung either over a bowl or on a tree limb until all the whey had drained out. Next, the remaining cheese was salted lightly and mixed with a small amount of the cream which had been skimmed from the milk. For the variety of cottage cheese which my family preferred, the milk was warmed to about 110° and then drained. (In case you don't have a cheese thermometer, the milk should feel warm to your wrist—rather like a baby's formula.) The cheese was then finished in the same way as above. The heated cheese had a much firmer curd, which I prefer. I should warn you that if you get it too warm, the curd will have the consistency (and flavor) of a piece of rubber.

In addition to cottage cheese, I think of **new potatoes** with green peas. Potatoes were also planted early. Since they must be grown in very soft, loose soil, it was very easy to "gravel" out a few small potatoes along the side of each plant without hurting the plant. These small, new potatoes were then boiled whole, buttered, and served with spring peas. They were also served with cream and butter or in a simple cream sauce. Later, in "Summer," we will see new potatoes appear with fresh green beans.

One last word about peas. An old-time favorite was peas with dumplings. Now, in my heart I know that peas with dumplings makes no sense at all. In fact, though, the combination is very good. Somehow, I think of this as something we had with canned peas—something we had when there was not much else to have. But I am assured by any number of people who are in a position to know that this is simply an old prejudice of mine. In the interest of fairness, I include

Peas with Dumplings

3 cups cooked peas (or 1 17-ounce
   can of peas undrained)
4 tablespoons butter
1 quart whole milk (or water)
dumplings (see below)
salt to taste

Place peas, butter, and milk into a large, heavy Dutch oven. Bring to a hard boil. Drop dumplings into the boiling liquid slowly enough so that the liquid remains at a hard boil. When all the dumplings have been added, reduce the heat, cover, and cook without uncovering for 15 minutes at low heat. Uncover and stir gently. If not thick, allow to cook uncovered until thick (no more than 5 additional minutes). Add salt to taste. Serve hot.

Dumplings

2 cups all-purpose flour
2 teaspoons baking powder
½ teaspoon salt

⅓ cup solid shortening
¾ cup milk

Add baking powder and salt to flour and mix thoroughly. Cut in shortening until completely mixed. Blend in milk until a stiff dough is formed. Knead fully, working in more flour if necessary to form a very stiff dough. Roll thin on a well-floured board and cut into strips about 2 inches wide. Pick up each strip of dough and tear off pieces about 2 inches square and drop the pieces into boiling liquid.

Another sure indication of spring was green onions. If you have a flower bed in full sun, you too can have fresh green onions. Simply buy some onion sets at your neighborhood gardening store and press them into lightly worked soil about half an inch apart. Stand back and wait. If you like your onions to have a lot of white, you just mound a little loose soil up around the onions as they grow. You can't miss. (You *really* can't miss if you just pick them up at the produce counter.)

Green onions are one part of that most delicious of spring and summer treats: wilted lettuce and onions. But most of the lettuce in the produce department of grocery stores is not tender enough for that dish. Fortunately, leaf lettuce is easy to grow. A number of good varieties are now available, but I still like the old-fashioned, black-seeded Simpson best. These seeds are easy to find at any gardening store and are also easy to grow, though only in cool weather. So you can plant it in a flower bed in the early spring, and it will be gone by the time you want to put in annuals. And with the right lettuce and onions you can have

Wilted Lettuce with Green Onions

Wash thoroughly and drain and dry 4 to 6 cups of fresh leaf lettuce and tear the leaves into 3 or 4 pieces each. Place in a heat-proof bowl. Cut 4 or 5 fresh green onions crosswise into thin slices and place on top of the lettuce. Salt lightly. Fry 4 or 5 slices of either salt or commercial bacon until crisp. Remove the bacon from the grease and heat the grease until smoking hot. Pour the hot grease and ½ cup cider vinegar over the lettuce at the same time. Toss the lettuce and onions with the hot vinegar and oil and serve immediately. Sprinkle the crumbled bacon over the lettuce and onions, if you like.

There are many variations on this classic salad. Some people add the vinegar to the hot oil before pouring it over the greens, while others heat the vinegar separately; still others pour the grease over the greens first, then warm the vinegar in the same hot skillet. " 'Everybody to their own notion,' said the old lady as she kissed the cow."

Consider this a bonus. For a wonderful taste, substitute **fresh spinach** for the lettuce in classic wilted salad. It has a fine taste and texture, and the color is lovely.

Wilted lettuce was as close to salad as we came. Fresh radishes and green onions or simply raw white onions were served with meals as were cucumbers later in the season, but these foods more often tended to be cooked or pickled. Radishes, planted early in the spring and at intervals throughout the summer, were a standard part of a meal. Both the round red varieties and the much hotter long white varieties were served.

If you will indulge me just a bit further, let me establish a couple of things about what gardens meant when I was growing up. First, most of the work of planting a garden in the two families that I knew best was left to the women and children of the family. In the spring, the men would plow, disk, and rake the garden. They would perhaps even lay it off in rows. Then they left it alone.

The care and maintenance of such a country garden was no easy task. In both the Dossett and the Weaver households, the main garden was close to an acre. At the Weavers', the garden was just across a small back yard from the kitchen entrance to the house. At the end nearest the house, there was an old-fashioned picket fence gate which led through the wire fence into the garden. Just inside this fence, Granny Weaver had planted rhubarb and perennial flowers—mostly larkspurs, as I remember. Just outside the fence in the back yard were hollyhocks. They almost hid the garden from view, even though it was no more than ten feet from the kitchen window.

At Mammy Dossett's, the garden was across a fairly large field, which was used to grow hay. Therefore, to get to the garden, it was necessary to walk beyond the barn to a roadway that led back through the orchard to the garden. In each case, my relatives knew exactly what they wanted in their garden and when they wanted it planted. While the garden at Mammy Dossett's was fairly new, the one at the Weavers' had been used as a garden for fifty years by the time I came along. It had been plowed and covered with manure from the barns and replowed so many times that you could stick a hoe all the way into the ground by just dropping it. No wonder things grew so well.

Another important part of spring was Easter. In fact, much of country life in East Tennessee revolved around the calendar of the church. With Easter, as with so many other holidays, food played an important role. I still have a great picture of myself standing in the side yard at my great-grandmother's and wearing my new Easter suit, which Ma Freeman had bought for me; my grandmother is holding a coconut cake, which the two of us obviously admire.

With Easter, I think of coconut cake (which we'll discuss in the last chapter, "Good Stuff") and ham and, of course, eggs. In the country, you always had plenty of eggs. You ate them fried, scrambled, and boiled. At Easter, you ate them lots of other ways as well. I can remember our boiling and dying two or three dozen eggs for church Easter egg hunts on Saturday afternoon and for family egg hunts on Easter Day. Since they were usually brown eggs, the hues tended to be somewhat subdued, but I loved them anyway. For a couple of weeks before Easter, we would carefully pick through the eggs, selecting those that were smoothest and lightest in color and placing them in a separate basket. Mammy Dossett explained that it didn't matter that we kept them so long because older eggs peeled easier when they were boiled. Interestingly enough, that is one of the few advantages to eggs these days. They are rarely fresh enough for peeling to be a problem.

Because the eggs would sometimes break in the boiling, a few extras were always added. I remember that we almost always had store-bought dye but my grandmothers and great-grandmother would always talk about how they dyed eggs with natural dyes when they were small. I remember their saying that onion skins made yellow and that hickory bark made a different yellow and that walnut hulls made a strange green (I think) and that some kind of corncobs made red. I still love to dye Easter eggs and can almost always find some children who will humor me enough to let me "help" them.

Since food on the farm was not to be wasted, all those eggs had to be eaten. That meant just eggs, deviled eggs, goldenrod eggs, creamed eggs, egg salad, and then more just eggs if necessary. I don't even want to talk about how a country school room smelled on the Monday after Easter—I mean from all the eggs in all the lunch bags, of course. In honor of all those Easters, I will give you a few egg recipes.

First you need **hard-cooked eggs**. Put the eggs in a large container and cover them with cold water; then place the pan on medium heat and allow the water to come just to a boil. Simmer about ten minutes for eggs that are hard cooked. Drain off the hot water and immediately cover the eggs with cold water. After allowing them to stand for a couple of minutes, again drain off the water and cover them again with cold water. By this time the eggs should be cool enough to handle, and you can proceed with dying or peeling or whatever your heart desires. By the way, if you plan to dye the eggs, it is better not to use an aluminum pot. The aluminum will leave some sort of deposit at the point the egg rubs against the pot, which will dye the egg a darker color.

Deviled Eggs

6 hard-cooked eggs	1 teaspoon salad mustard
3 tablespoons mayonnaise	1 teaspoon salt

Cut eggs in half lengthwise and remove the yolks, being careful not to break the whites. In a small bowl, blend yolks, mayonnaise, mustard, and salt thoroughly. The mixture should be smooth and firm enough to hold its shape. If it is too firm, add more mayonnaise; if too soft, add another egg yolk. Stuff the yolk mixture back into the egg whites, mounding it slightly. Serve cold.

To these basic deviled eggs you can add finely chopped pickle relish, finely chopped celery, or even capers (though Harbison's Crossroads hadn't heard much about things like capers). However, I take mine straight.

Egg salad is simply deviled eggs for the lazy. Instead of separating the eggs, simply chop the white and the yolk finely together. Add enough mayonnaise (about 4 tablespoons for 6 eggs) and mustard (about 2 teaspoons for 6 eggs) to moisten them and add salt and pepper to taste. I use about a teaspoon of salt and a good sprinkle of pepper. This mixture makes a lovely sandwich filling but should not be kept unrefrigerated for very long.

Goldenrod eggs take a bit more work. My mother learned to make goldenrod eggs in a home economics class at Gibbs High School, and I still think of these eggs as something special. Even though I almost never take the time to do them correctly, I do remember them fondly.

Goldenrod Eggs

6 hard-cooked eggs,	1 cup milk
peeled and separated	salt and pepper to taste
3 tablespoons butter	6 slices good white bread,
2 tablespoons flour	toasted

Prepare a white sauce by melting the butter in a heavy saucepan. Keep the heat low enough that the butter will not brown. Blend in the flour, stirring constantly, and continue to cook for two or three minutes. Add the milk and continue to stir constantly until the mixture boils and is thick. Add salt and pepper. Chop the egg whites and stir them into the white sauce. Place each slice of toast on a serving plate and spoon the egg white mixture evenly over them. Sieve the egg yolks over each in a pleasing pattern and serve hot.

I usually simply prepare a double recipe of the white sauce and carefully stir egg slices or even egg halves or quarters into it. Goldenrod eggs is a great dish to serve with cold, baked country ham and a fruit compote for an elegant breakfast. If you really want to impress folks with these eggs, stir about 4 ounces of inexpensive American cheese and about a half teaspoon of salad mustard into the white sauce and allow the cheese to melt before adding the eggs.

Enough about eggs. (But this isn't to say that eggs won't continue to be important throughout the year in the country kitchen.)

Much has been written and said about family structure, and sociologists worry about matriarch and patriarch and who controlled and the role of children and parents. But one small happening in my family is all I have ever needed to understand the true nature of these things. I have already introduced you to Granny and Grandpa Weaver. Although they would be considered poor by today's standards, they were proud, independent people who believed in looking after their own needs. Every Saturday, Grandpa went into Knoxville to sell butter and eggs and vegetables and whatever else he had available to customers along a "route" he had established. I was often allowed to go along.

Grandpa Weaver was a gruff, distant man who always gave the impression that he expected everyone to do whatever he said. Most of us did. Granny, in contrast, was an extremely quiet, kind woman who usually gave the impression of doing whatever she was told. On one particular Saturday morning, she mentioned that she didn't have enough hens making nests and "setting" to have enough baby chicks, so she wanted him to buy some when he went into Knoxville. He thereupon informed her that he had no intention of spending money for baby chicks because she was too impatient to wait for the hens to do what they were supposed to. She said nothing more until we were just ready to leave. Standing at the end of the front porch near the car, she said quietly, "Mr. Weaver, bring back those chickens." He said nothing. All the way home that afternoon, the peeping of those chickens in their box in the back seat with me helped me understand the working of things in a well-regulated country home.

While I'm thinking about the Weavers, I can't help remembering something else about Grandpa Weaver. Any interest I have in the world of politics and my insatiable need to read newspapers, I trace to Grandpa. I knew him only in his old age, but what I remember most was that he read. He would come in from the fields on a hot summer day and get the Knoxville *Journal* from the mailbox (where it had been placed in same-day delivery from the post office) and sit in the swing on the front porch and read. If I were around, he would read to me. I didn't know what this essentially unschooled man was reading about most of the time, but I knew the reading had value. I still believe that. I don't share his conviction that all truth is to be found in the Knoxville *Journal*, the Bible, and the Book of Discipline of the Methodist Church (in that order, I think), but I do like to read.

April and May brought the first fruits of the season and with them wonderful treats. My favorite was and still is **fried apples**. This wonderful dish needs early transparent, or one of the other thin-skinned, sour early apples, but is simple to prepare.

Wash, core and remove any blemishes, and slice thin about eight or ten small, green cooking apples. Do not peel. Heat about four tablespoons of butter (or margarine) in a heavy skillet with a tight-fitting lid. When the butter is melted and bubbly, add the apples, stir, and place over low heat, covered, to cook slowly. Stir occasionally until the apples start to cook up (that is, start to fall apart). Remove the cover, add one cup sugar, and stir thoroughly. Allow to cook uncovered, stirring as needed to prevent sticking, until thick and starting to brown. Serve either hot or cold.

I find that Granny Smith apples work fairly well in making fried apples. I do think the peels are a little tough, so I usually peel them, but they have a nice tart taste similar to the more traditional apples. I am also happy to report that there is an increased interest in growing the traditional apples. My mother's three trees in her suburban back yard provide apples for her whole big family. (These old-fashioned apples freeze nicely, too.)

Fried apples most often appeared at breakfast, although they could be a part of almost any meal. We might as well pause here a minute to talk about the institution of the country breakfast. When these folks broke their fast, they broke it completely. Breakfast would always include biscuits and some kind of cured pork. That might be salt bacon, or sausage (either canned or fresh), or even ham or shoulder. Some kind of gravy, either milk gravy or red-eye gravy, would almost certainly be included. Cooked cereal —usually old-fashioned oatmeal, rice, or cornmeal mush—was fairly common. Fried or scrambled eggs were almost universal. In summer, fried corn and tomatoes might be part of breakfast. Hot cakes and syrup were also served fairly often. In fact, this might be as good a place as any to tell you how to make hot cakes and even homemade syrup in case you have a sudden craving and the convenience store is closed.

Hot Cakes

3 cups flour	¼ cup shortening
1 tablespoon baking powder	2 eggs
1 teaspoon salt	1½ cups milk
¼ cup sugar	shortening or butter for frying

In a large mixing bowl, stir together the flour, salt, baking powder, and sugar. Work in the shortening until the mixture has the texture of fine cornmeal. Form a well in the center of the mixture and add the milk into which you have beaten the eggs. Mix just until thoroughly blended. The mixture should have the consistency of very heavy cream.

Lightly grease a griddle which has been heated to medium hot. Pour the hot cake mixture onto the hot griddle. About ¼ cup will make a very large hot cake. I prefer about 3 tablespoons for a somewhat smaller cake. If you want silver dollars, make the batter a little thinner and use about a tablespoonful. Remember, you are in charge here. When bubbles show through the cake and it starts to brown around the edges, turn it over and brown the other side. If the cake reaches this stage very quickly, your pan is probably too hot. Continue to grease the pan lightly between each set of hot cakes and continue frying until all are cooked. Serve hot.

Country Syrup

3 cups sugar

⅓ cup water

1 teaspoon maple extract

Mix the sugar and water in a heavy saucepan. Place on the stove over medium heat and bring to a full boil. Stir in the maple extract. Serve hot.

By the first week in May, strawberries started to be available, and they were delicious (though much smaller and much sourer than today's berries). In the orchard, we even had a patch of wild strawberries that were wonderful. In case you didn't know, wild strawberries that are safe to eat have a white bloom. A strawberry-like weed with a yellow bloom also grows in this area, but its berry is inedible.

Commercial strawberries, especially Tennessee Beauties, were a fairly common cash crop for the spring. I remember going to a neighbor's house with my father and mother when I was very small and helping them prepare strawberries for the Knoxville market. In those days, wooden strawberry boxes were filled with berries and prime large berries were then arranged to make an even top layer for the box. As I remember, it was called "topping off" the box. I know that it took a lot of time just for appearance's sake. I also know that Maggie Bright, who owned the strawberry fields, allowed people to come in and pick their own for a much smaller price than those she sold in Knoxville. (You probably thought that pick-your-own farms were a new development.)

For a wonderful addition to breakfast, strawberries were most often just capped, sliced, covered with sugar, and allowed to stand overnight. They were also served as shortcake. This shortcake, made in the true English tradition which the earliest settlers to this area brought with them, is still my favorite, although I usually take a shortcut and make strawberry shortcake with pound cake.

Traditional Shortcake

2 cups plain flour
½ cup butter
½ cup sugar
1 tablespoon baking powder
1 teaspoon salt
1 cup milk

Blend flour, sugar, baking powder, and salt. Cut in butter with a pastry blender or a fork until well mixed. Stir in milk to form a firm dough. Turn out onto a floured board and knead lightly for a few turns. Flatten onto the board and roll into an oval about ½ inch thick. Fold over and reroll to ½ inch thick. Cut with a biscuit cutter and place carefully onto an ungreased baking sheet with the edges not touching. Reroll and cut any scraps until all the dough has been used. Bake in a 375° oven about 15 minutes or until lightly browned. Remove from the oven and brush the tops lightly with melted butter and sprinkle with sugar. Allow to cool to room temperature. To serve, split the shortbreads and fill with sliced, sugared strawberries, which have been refrigerated overnight. Top with additional strawberries and lightly whipped cream.

What I'm about to admit is heresy of the worst kind. I'm not crazy about strawberry preserves—I find them far too sweet and sticky. (I do find the new varieties of uncooked preserves are passable, but even they are loaded with sugar, so I try to avoid them.) However, I realize that I am almost alone in this opinion, and to appease all those folks who rhapsodize about strawberry preserves on hot biscuits, I give you what Louise Durman, food editor of the Knoxville *News-Sentinel*, tells me is their single most requested recipe of all time:

Lucy Curtis Templeton's Strawberry Preserves

1 quart strawberries, washed and stemmed

3 cups sugar

Put 1½ cups sugar with fruit in pan and boil 5 minutes. Add remaining sugar and boil 10 to 15 minutes. A watery fruit must be cooked longer. Pour into an earthenware jar, a wide-mouthed glass jar, or a ceramic container. Do *not* use metal. Let stand 24 hours. Stir occasionally. If using soon, store in refrigerator. If not, pour into sterilized jars and process or freeze. (The U.S. Department of Agriculture recommends processing in a hot-water bath for 5 minutes.) The small amount of fruit and the short cooking time are always cited as the secret of these preserves. Accordingly, the recipe should *not* be doubled before cooking.

I'm saving most of the desserts for later, but with the arrival of apples, strawberries, gooseberries, grapes, rhubarb, and the whole array of spring and summer fruits, I've at least got to mention the subject of fruit pies. The tart, sweet flavor of fruits and berries baked in a crust and served with fresh cream is almost irresistible. (If you just can't wait, skip ahead to "Good Stuff.")

Thoughts of cool, fresh cream remind me how essential milk and milk products were to our good country food. Sweet milk—to drink and to cook with—had a role in every meal. Buttermilk was almost as common. Butter contributed its special flavor to a multitude of recipes as well as to direct (and lavish) applications on bread or potatoes or sweet potatoes or cinnamon toast or any number of other things. (To make cinnamon toast the old way, you take half a biscuit and butter it generously. Then you sprinkle it with sugar and cinnamon and put it in a hot oven until the sugar and butter melt. If you happen to be very hungry, just leave out the oven part and when you have finished spreading and sprinkling, just eat it. Later we'll talk more about biscuits and leftover biscuits.)

One interesting side effect of having cows was having feed sack materials for clothes. Now I'm not talking about wearing burlap bags à la Erskine Caldwell. I'm talking about the custom of packing cow feed and chicken feed in fairly good cotton cloth bags which were made to come easily apart. Since these were 100-pound bags, you got fairly good-sized pieces of cloth. By selecting feed in matching bags, you could get enough for a dress or a shirt. If I remember correctly, smaller quantities of feed were sometimes packed in already completed pillow cases. At any rate, every woman I knew had a sewing machine and could turn these feed bags into serviceable clothes; scraps could be made into quilts. Remember that Scottish ancestry!

But we were talking about milk. As essential as it was, it had one major drawback. Milk comes from cows. Actually, it doesn't come; you have to take it. You have to take it every morning and

every night. Even when it is cold. Even when it is hot. Even when you can think of a thousand other things that would be more fun than milking a cow, it still has to be done. The tyranny of a cow needing to be milked is complete. And despite what this generation may believe about the nobility of the rural life, there is no nobility in milking a cow that is not all that wild about being milked. Cows tend to be surly. They have been known to kick. They always find it delightful to hit you repeatedly across the face with tails that have been places that make them decidedly unpleasant. Cows smell awful. If you milk them, you smell awful. But it's almost worth it to have all the cold milk, butter, cream, and even buttermilk you want, not to mention cottage cheese.

Country folks attached great importance to having cows and

milk. Even when Mammy Dossett was in her mid-seventies, widowed again and growing increasingly unable to live alone and take care of herself, she fought to the very end to be allowed to keep a cow. Somehow that seemed to be essential to her independence.

Even though cows were held to be really important, that didn't make them any more pleasant to deal with. I don't like cows. (I also hate chickens, but everything in its own time.)

3
Summer

For small farmers like my kinfolks, summer meant hard work. Spring and summer were given to plowing, planting, hoeing, gathering, drying, and canning—in addition to doing all the other chores which were part of everyday life year-round. (And my old enemies, the cows, were always present.) Besides food for people, it was necessary to raise food for the animals, and that meant corn, wheat and hay. Then (as now), tobacco was raised as a major cash crop. All this fieldwork had to be done while the sun was shining, and it was done without modern machinery. I'm not crying poor mouth when I tell you that I was a teenager when we first bought a tractor. It's not that we were deprived—I didn't know three people who had one. You plowed, planted, and did whatever else needed to be done with a team of horses (or, God help you, mules) and the tools they could operate.

You have to understand how we worked to understand how we ate. People worked very hard; although they ate large quantities of high-energy foods, they seldom got fat. But if we persist today in eating the same amounts of foods prepared in the same way, it will be *fat city*. I haven't allowed for this in my life. I have always maintained a lifestyle which permits me to keep my weight in a closely controlled range: I never allow it to go below two hundred pounds or above three hundred. Through years of research I've discovered that if I'm to stay anywhere near the bottom of this range, I must treat most foods of my childhood as rewards for good behavior rather than as a normal diet. In most cases they simply don't lend themselves to defatting, desugaring, or unbuttering. Sorry about that!

The eating habits of my kinfolks differed from those of modern city-dwellers in another significant way. While we had three meals a day, and sometimes (most times) a bedtime snack, our overall pattern of eating was different and that difference led to a different terminology for meals. Today, we have breakfast, lunch, and dinner. In those days, we had breakfast, dinner, and supper. All this is to say that the big meals of the day used to be in the morning and at mid-day. The evening meal was likely to be much lighter and in many cases was food which had been cooked at mid-day and was served cold.

I believe that this pattern of meals reflected two important facets of our lifestyle. One was related to the hard physical work in barns and fields. If you followed a plow and a team of horses all morning, you needed a substantial breakfast. If you were going to follow them again all afternoon, the mid-day meal needed to be even more substantial. The other related to the conditions with which farm wives had to cope. Finishing the cooking by mid-day allowed them to escape from the wood-burning stove and turn to other tasks in the afternoon.

It wasn't just being old-fashioned that led us to call our meals breakfast, dinner, and supper. We knew that among civilized folks the big meal of the day, whenever it is served, is dinner and a light meal served in the evening is supper. And that's what we had.

This might be as good a time as any to talk a little about talk. I am greatly put off by those folks who attempt to catch East Tennessee dialect in print. Somehow "hit" for "it" can sound perfectly normal when you hear it all your life but appear illiterate when set down in black and white. Mammy Dossett felt "right piert" or "plum tuckered." She went down the road "a piece" and if she had time, she would "red up" the house. All this had a naturalness which I now remember as almost lyrical, but when I was younger, listening to these expressions was something of a trial for me.

I still remember coming back after my time at Yale to visit with my grandmother and her husband in the house where I had been born. I had visited with Dad Dossett and their neighbor on the front porch for a while. Then I had gone into the living room to read. The windows were open. As I sat there all sophisticated and learned, I heard the neighbor say, "Jim, that boy has been off up there to that fancy school all this time and he just talks like everybody else, don't he?" I'm not sure how I could have been so devastated then and feel so pleased now about the same thing.

A couple of other things might also help you understand how my folks talked. Mammy used a very simple system to get to brag about any of her grandchildren. She would first say something which was sort of loosely critical. "Well, I finally got my grandson to come out and pay some attention to his grandmother," she would say. This statement could then be followed by the most blatant of compliments. "You probably hadn't heard that he's been chosen to rule the world" would be a completely acceptable follow-up statement. But we can't just "set around" here talking all day. We have work to do.

Summer didn't mean hard work alone; it also meant the pleasures of fresh vegetables. One of the great losses in restaurants in this country for many years was the disappearance of good vegetables of the sort I remember from the summers of my boyhood. Thank God, really good restaurants have rediscovered, reintroduced, and often improved on traditional ways of serving them. Have you ever had lightly boiled carrots sautéd in butter with leeks? An absolute delight. We didn't have those in Corryton, though. We did have fried okra, green beans, corn, sliced tomatoes, and cornbread and were well off. If you added fried apples,

pickled beets, baked acorn squash, and topped it off with apple cobbler and a glass of cold milk, you were in heaven.

Of all the vegetables of summer, perhaps the most important is corn. Corn and beans, traditionally planted on Good Friday, became available fairly early in summer. At its simplest, corn was pulled, shucked, boiled, and eaten. It was eaten with lots of butter and salt, and it was good. Purists argued that boiled corn should always be cooked the same day it was pulled. Fanatics said you should have a pot at the end of the row with the water boiling before you pulled the corn. Everyone agrees that as corn stands the natural sugar in the corn is converted to starch and the corn is not so good. The corn we had back then was Hickory King and had to be eaten fairly young if it was not to be too hard. Modern varieties are much more forgiving and on the whole sweeter and better. The one thing that I am sure is better now than then is **boiled corn**. We no longer boil it at all. We clean the corn, place it in a covered casserole, and cook it on high in the microwave until it starts to look transparent. Butter and serve.

Of course, we weren't limited to boiled corn. Fried corn was also a major treat. I'm sure you know already that fried corn—or creamed corn, if you prefer—must be cut so fine that it is necessary to cut down each ear four times in each place to get all the corn. You then scrape the cob to get the last of the milk. If you can't cut it that fine yet, remember that practice makes perfect.

Fried Corn

6 ears of fresh corn

2 tablespoons butter

salt to taste

Cut the corn finely from the cob and scrape the cobs. Melt the butter in a heavy saucepan and add the corn. Keep the heat low and cook the corn slowly, stirring often for about fifteen minutes. Salt to taste. Be careful! Corn sticks quickly and burns just as quickly. Burned corn tastes awful.

Many people used bacon grease rather than butter to fry corn. If that is your preference, fry three strips of either commercial or salt bacon until crisp. Remove and reserve. Cook the corn in the grease and crumble the bacon over the corn just before you serve it.

Some people will tell you that you should add sugar to fried corn. Fine. Add about the same amount of sugar as you do salt. In fairness, I have to say that if the corn is good enough and fresh enough, you don't need sugar.

Many folks also thought that fried corn should have black pepper in it. This was especially true for corn cooked in bacon fat. Those same people put pepper on boiled corn. Try it. You might like it, but I doubt it.

Leftover fried corn was the basis for one of my favorite dishes. I discovered later that some people called it Indian pudding. I thought it was baked corn pudding. Whatever its name, it is good. (It can also be made quite well from canned cream-style corn, but don't tell anyone I told you.)

Corn Pudding

2 cups cold fried corn (or a 17-ounce can of cream-style)	2 tablespoons plain flour
1 cup whole milk	2 eggs
	2 tablespoons sugar

Blend flour into corn; add milk, beaten eggs, and sugar. Pour into a buttered 1-quart casserole and bake at 350° about 30 minutes or until just firm in the center. Serve hot, warm, or at room temperature.

What people called this and other dishes is an interesting matter itself. Talking about this recently with someone who knows far more about the subject than I do, I asked her what she thought Indian pudding was and she described the dish above. Phila Hach, who was in the same group, disagreed, saying that this was corn pudding. Later she sent me the following recipe for Indian pudding.

Phila Hach's
Indian Pudding

1 tablespoon butter
½ cup boiling water
2 quarts milk
2 cups yellow cornmeal

1 teaspoon salt
1 cup dark molasses
¼ teaspoon ground ginger

Rub the butter around the bottom of a deep kettle. When melted, add the boiling water. Put in 1 quart of the milk and let it boil up. Stir in the cornmeal and salt. Stir until thick and set aside to cool. When cool, add the molasses, ginger, and the other quart of milk to the cooled mush. Pour into a deep baking dish and bake covered in a 275° oven for 10 to 12 hours. (Yes, really and truly 10 to 12 hours! This dish requires a long cooking time and a relatively low temperature.) Serve warm with thick, cold cream.

Phila, whom we will talk more about later, tells me that this is a true old New England recipe. But with those ingredients, it could just as easily be an East Tennessee dish.

Talking about corn seems to lead me naturally into talking about okra. What you think about okra is a major cultural indicator. If you ask what it is, you are probably from the North or Far West. If you think it is principally an ingredient to thicken soup, you are probably from Louisiana. If you think it is grown to pickle, you are probably from Texas. If you are willing to eat it any way it is served, including boiled and buttered, you are probably from East Tennessee and more than fifty. I fall into the final category (with some reservations). I prefer it fried in the traditional manner. I like it pickled. I find it an interesting addition to soup, and if I haven't eaten in two days, boiled and buttered is fine.

Fried Okra

1 pound tender young okra	4 tablespoons bacon fat
½ cup plain cornmeal	(or cooking oil)
salt to taste	

Cut the okra crosswise into ¼-inch slices. Pour the cornmeal over the okra and stir to mix. Heat the oil in a well-seasoned iron skillet until a single piece of the okra dropped into it sizzles. Add the okra, and stir to coat with the oil. Don't worry if the okra absorbs all the oil—if the skillet is well seasoned, the okra won't stick. Cover and cook, stirring occasionally, until the okra changes color and starts to be tender. Remove the lid and increase the heat, stirring often until the okra is browned. Salt to taste.

Today, most okra is served French fried. If you like it that way, my advice is to have it at a country restaurant. I do like it cooked the following way.

French Fried Whole Okra

½ pound young, small	1 egg
(1- to 1½-inch) okra	milk to make a thick batter
½ cup cornmeal mix	(about ¼ cup)

Thoroughly wash and dry the pods of okra and leave them whole, including the stem. Mix together the cornmeal mix, egg, and milk to make a thick batter. Dip okra into the batter and drop individually into hot oil at least 1 inch deep in a heavy, deep pan. Fry in batches until brown.

Note. The cornmeal mix has salt in it, so you probably don't need to add any more salt.

Pickled okra, though not traditional in our area, is good, so I include this recipe as a bonus.

Pickled Okra

3 to 4 pounds okra	1 quart white vinegar
4 small pods of hot red pepper	1 cup water
4 cloves garlic	½ cup salt (uniodized)

Wash the okra and pack the whole pods into hot, sterilized pint jars (I use wide-mouthed pints both because it is easier and because the pods can be put in upright and will look better). Place a pod of pepper and a clove of garlic in each jar. Heat vinegar, water, and salt to a boil and fill each jar. Seal immediately. Wait at least 2 weeks before serving.

Variation. Leave out the pepper and garlic and add a sprig of fresh dill or a teaspoon of dill seeds to each jar instead.

Okra was also used in soup and, in fact, corn, okra, and tomatoes were often canned together to make "soup mix." This combination was also often served on its own. We'll talk about soup when we get to next winter, but now's the time to cook these vegetables fresh.

Corn, Okra, and Tomatoes

4 ears of fresh corn (or 2 to 3 cups of leftover corn)	3 to 4 tablespoons butter or bacon grease
4 to 6 whole tomatoes	salt to taste
1 pound okra	

Peel the tomatoes, remove the seeds, and cut into small pieces. Cut the washed and dried okra crosswise into ¼-inch pieces. Cut the corn off the ears. Heat the butter or grease in a heavy saucepan and add the okra. Stir to coat and add the tomatoes. Continue to cook and to stir until boiling. Add the corn. Reduce the heat and cook slowly until the vegetables are cooked through and thick. Salt to taste. If using cooked corn, allow the tomatoes and okra to cook about 5 minutes before adding the corn.

Making **soup mix** requires only minor changes to the recipe. Use the ingredients listed above *except* the butter, mixed together and cooked lightly. Then pack the hot mixture into hot, sterilized jars. Add about 1 teaspoon salt and 1 tablespoon vinegar to the top of each quart. Seal each jar with new two-piece lids and process in a water bath canner or, preferably, a pressure cooker for the times recommended by the canner.

A word of caution. Home canned foods are wonderful, but proper canning is essential to avoid contaminated food. You have to be particularly careful with low acid foods, and this is the reason for the addition of vinegar in the preceding recipe. Foods very high in acid or sugar (pickles, jelly, jam, or preserves) are easy and safe to can. Be safe, not sorry.

If you don't want to cook okra in a mixture, you can make

Stewed Okra

1 pound okra	2 tablespoons butter
1 cup water	salt to taste
1 tablespoon cider vinegar	

Wash the okra and place in a saucepan with the water and the vinegar. Cover, bring to a boil, and cook until tender. Drain and stir in the butter and salt to taste.

Boiled okra tastes very good, but it has an absolutely awful texture—slick and nearly slimy. If that doesn't bother you, you'll love stewed okra.

Green beans are a true sign that summer has come. By the middle of June, the first green beans of the season are ready. When I was very young, a wide variety of beans were grown. I guess my favorite still is white half-runners, although there are many good varieties. Of course, pole beans like Kentucky Wonder were often planted in the cornfield. Whatever the variety, beans were almost always cooked the same way.

Country Green Beans

3 pounds green beans	salt to taste
salt pork	1 cup water

Wash the green beans; then string and break them into pieces about an inch long. Wash again. Place in a pot with a tight-fitting lid. Add a piece of salt pork about 4 inches long and about ½ inch thick, cut almost through to the skin in several places, and about one cup water. (The amount of water will vary depending on your pan. This is enough if the lid fits tightly. If not, you may need a little more.) Bring to a boil, reduce the heat, and allow to simmer for a couple of hours until the beans are tender, stirring occasionally. If water is still more than ½ inch deep in the bottom of the kettle, remove the lid and allow the excess water to boil away. Add salt to taste and serve hot.

I fully realize that this method of cooking sends modern nutritionists into fits. I'm sorry. There is no other authentic way. Just to make them feel better, I'll tell you that fresh green beans can be cut in the French manner and stir-fried quickly in about a tablespoon of hot oil with about a tablespoon of soy sauce added at the end for a lovely (but unauthentic) side dish.

Green beans were an important part of the diet year-round from the very earliest days. Traditionally they were preserved by drying, which I can still recommend for a different taste. In more recent times they have been canned. Many vegetables can be canned quite adequately commercially; however, this does not include green beans. For many years, one of our most cherished Christmas gifts has been the jars of green beans which my mother cans in a pressure canner. We guard them carefully, since they're almost as good as fresh. If you intend to can beans, I urge you to buy a good pressure canner and follow the instructions to the letter. As beans are particularly low in acid, it is critical to take adequate precautions in canning them. Further, home-canned beans should never, *never,* be eaten without boiling them thoroughly. Canned green beans are worth the effort, but it's even better if you can find someone who will give them to you. Good luck!

Dried green beans, another country tradition, are much less tricky. To dry green beans, you can either prepare and break them exactly as if you were going to cook them or you can string them and leave the beans whole. If you want to leave them whole, you can string them up on a heavy sewing thread pulled crosswise through the center of the beans. Each string can be as long as you like but is most manageable about 2 to 3 feet long. I prefer to break the beans. Spread the broken beans on a clean white cloth on a table in full sun for at least 4 or 5 days, bringing them in at night—you can just pick up the corners of the cloth and allow the beans to remain in it. The next morning simply spread the cloth back out and distribute the beans evenly over it. After the first couple of days of drying, when the beans wrapped in the cloth are brought in, they can be placed in an oven which has been warmed and turned off. Well-dried beans will rattle when shaken in the cloth. To store the beans, place them in a clean white cloth bag and hang it in a cool, dark, dry place.

To cook dried green beans, wash them thoroughly, cover with water, allow to soak overnight, and then drain. Add water and salt pork as for fresh beans. Bring to a boil, then reduce the heat and cook a couple of hours or until reasonably tender. Instead of salt pork, bacon grease can be used; if so, it should be added when the beans are almost finished cooking.

Don't expect dried beans to have exactly the same texture

or taste as fresh ones. They tend to be much darker in color and to retain a certain toughness when cooked. Nevertheless, I like both the taste and texture of dried beans. Fortunately, they are reasonably easy to dry—try them yourself.

By midsummer, we started to have tomatoes and cucumbers. I'm not sure why I mention the two of these together except that I think of them together. For most of the year, I eat tomatoes only if they are cooked. Most commercially grown tomatoes ship very well; it's a shame they can't have some flavor. In summer, however, when *real* tomatoes are available, they are wonderful. Though I personally have a preference for yellow tomatoes, I'll eat any fresh vine-ripened tomato with great pleasure. They are delightful simply sliced and eaten with fresh fried corn. Traditionally, they were served at all three meals—they are excellent with breakfast foods, including biscuits and gravy. (As I mentioned in "Spring," fried corn was also often served with breakfast. That is not to my taste, but on a lazy Sunday morning it can be an interesting addition to brunch.)

If you remember, I told you earlier that we were rural but not completely so. Tomatoes bring to mind one great proof of that. Summer is not summer without tomato sandwiches. When I was growing up they were made with cold biscuits. Later commercial white breads took the place of the biscuits. If you see me eating a sandwich made with that insubstantial white stuff which now generally passes for sandwich bread, you can be sure that there are slices of fresh tomato between the slices of bread. In case you don't know, a proper tomato sandwich consists of slices of ripe tomato, sprinkled liberally with salt and pepper, on white bread which has been generously spread with mayonnaise. If you insist, you may add fresh leaf lettuce or even a slice of good American cheese. But I'll take my tomato sandwiches straight.

Tomatoes were also cooked—both ripe and green. I suppose it is an ingrained prejudice, but I still don't have much use for barely cooked broiled tomatoes with a few crumbs and some butter on top. Tomatoes should be either raw or completely cooked. None of this lukewarm stuff for me. An old farm boy is more likely to have

Stewed Tomatoes

6 large tomatoes   4 tablespoons butter
¼ cup water   salt to taste

Peel the tomatoes and quarter them. Squeeze out excess seeds. Place the tomatoes and the water in a heavy saucepan, cover, and bring to a boil. Reduce the heat and cook slowly until tender. Add butter and salt. Stir and serve.

Now I admit that this basic recipe is pretty uninspired, but it allows you all sorts of leeway in seasoning the tomatoes. I suggest adding some chopped onion to the tomatoes at the beginning, or perhaps some chopped sweet basil. Such additions may not be traditional, but they surely improve the flavor. Stewed tomatoes are most useful as the basis for something else. In truth, I included stewed tomatoes only as an excuse to talk about one of the stranger and more tasty dishes native to this area.

Tomato Pudding

3 to 3½ cups cooked tomatoes   ½ cup water
  (or a 29-ounce can)   4 tablespoons butter
¾ cup sugar   4 to 6 cold biscuits

In a heavy saucepan, mix together the tomatoes, sugar, water and butter. Bring to a boil. Crumble the biscuits into the boiling tomato mixture, stirring constantly. Reduce the heat and continue to cook until thick, stirring often. Serve hot or at room temperature.

This strange-sounding mixture makes a nice side dish for roast pork or roast lamb. It can also be made with white yeast bread but is not as good as with leftover biscuits. It can also be cooked as above and then placed in a buttered casserole and baked until brown on top.

Tomatoes, canned in large quantities, appeared regularly on our table. They were served not just as stewed tomatoes or as tomato pudding but were an essential ingredient in the ever-present vegetable soup, a staple throughout the year. Although you may want to can tomatoes, I personally find commercially canned tomatoes just as good as I remember home-canned ones. And in "Winter," when we talk about recipes using canned tomatoes, I'll let you decide if you want to be a purist and only use home-canned ones. Of course, if you have even just a couple of tomato plants in your yard, you may have so many tomatoes that you have no choice but to can some. Homemade tomato juice is vastly superior to commercial varieties and is simple to make. It, too, is easy to can and makes a nice alternative to allowing extra tomatoes to rot on the window sill.

Tomato Juice

very ripe tomatoes (quantity doesn't matter—use what you have)
salt to taste (about 1 teaspoon per quart)

Wash the tomatoes and remove the hard core. Chop into large pieces in an appropriate kettle. *Add no water.* Bring slowly to a boil, stirring often. Cook until completely cooked up. Run through a colander (or a strainer if you do not have a colander), pressing hard to remove as much pulp as possible. Add salt to taste. Pour into hot sterilized jars and seal. Process in a water-bath canner for 10 to 15 minutes.

As I mentioned, you need not wait for tomatoes to ripen to eat them. Probably the most traditional way of serving green tomatoes was to fry them.

Fried Green Tomatoes

6 large green tomatoes   1 teaspoon salt
cornmeal   bacon grease for frying

Remove the core and slice the tomatoes crosswise into slices about ¼ inch thick. Sprinkle the salt lightly over the slices. Dip both sides of each slice into the cornmeal. Heat about 2 tablespoons bacon grease in a heavy skillet (remember, a well-seasoned cast-iron one is always best). Place as many slices into the skillet as will fit in a single layer and fry at medium heat until brown on the bottom. Turn and brown on the other side. Continue to fry in batches until all the slices are fried. If you like a thicker breading on fried green tomatoes, the slices can be dipped first into a beaten egg and then into the cornmeal.

Green tomatoes were also pickled. While they were done in a number of ways, my favorite is lime pickles. Please note that the "lime" here is pickling lime, which has absolutely nothing to do with the citrus fruit. Pickling lime is a corrosive chemical used in making pickles. Since pickling lime is still fairly easy to find in the canning section of supermarkets, I am able to include

Green Tomato Lime Pickles

7 pounds green tomatoes	2 quarts cider vinegar
2 cups pickling lime	8 cups sugar
2 gallons water	pickling spices to taste

Quarter the tomatoes or slice them (either works fine; it affects only the way they look) and place into a large container (*not* aluminum, which will react with the lime). Mix the lime and water together and pour over the tomatoes. Cover and allow to stand for 24 hours, stirring occasionally with a wooden spoon. Drain thoroughly and wash with 3 changes of cold water. Cover with water and allow to stand overnight (or at least 3 hours). Drain completely. Stir the vinegar and sugar together until the sugar is melted. Pour over the tomatoes and allow to stand overnight. Place in a non-aluminum kettle, add the pickling spices (I use about 2 tablespoons whole cloves, or you may use about the same amount of mixed pickling spices), bring to a boil, and allow to boil slowly for about 30 to 35 minutes. Pack into hot, sterilized jars and seal. Be sure that there is enough of the syrup in each jar to cover the tomatoes completely. This recipe will make about 6 to 8 pints.

Cucumber pickles can be made in exactly the same way, substituting sliced cucumbers for the green tomatoes. I have even made them using the firm flesh from large **zucchini,** though again we did not have zucchini in the Gibbs Community in the 1940s.

One of the more bizarre uses for green tomatoes was green tomato pie. I will tell you about it, and I think I even recommend it to you. At any rate, you might want to serve it on a slow night or when you want to impress everyone with how knowledgeable about American regional food you really are.

Green Tomato Pie

pie crust for a double-crust pie (see p. 175)

sliced green tomatoes

1 cup sugar

1 tablespoon flour

¾ teaspoon cinnamon

2 tablespoons vinegar

1 tablespoon water

2 tablespoons butter

Place the unbaked bottom crust in a deep 9-inch pie pan. Thinly slice enough green tomatoes to fill the crust. Combine sugar, flour, and cinnamon and spread evenly over the tomatoes. Sprinkle with the water and vinegar. Dot with the butter. Cover with the top crust and seal. Bake in a hot oven (400°) for 10 minutes. Reduce heat to 350° and cook for 25 to 30 minutes more or until brown.

Some time ago we started to talk about tomatoes and cucumbers, but so far we have talked about tomatoes with only a passing mention of cucumbers. I shouldn't slight them—fresh cucumbers were a summer staple. Although they were generally just cut up and served, they were also sometimes served in vinegar.

Fresh Cucumbers in Vinegar

fresh cucumber slices

onion slices

sugar

salt

vinegar

Place cucumber and onion slices in a glass, ceramic, or stainless steel container and sprinkle with about ¼ cup sugar and ½ teaspoon salt for each quart of vegetables. Cover with cider vinegar. Cover and allow to stand in the refrigerator for at least 4 hours or overnight. Serve cold. These will keep for several days in the refrigerator but are better when freshly made. (In penance for all the fat and sugar I have included in earlier recipes, I will tell you that these do very nicely using artificial sweetener instead of sugar and give you a food which is "free" if you are trying to watch your weight.)

When I was growing up, almost everyone made cucumber pickles, so I am going to include a couple of recipes, though, to be frank, I really don't like most homemade pickles. Bread and butter pickles are my favorites (rather, the ones I dislike least), and so we will start with them. In all of these pickles, it is important to use uniodized salt; otherwise, the pickles will turn dark.

Bread and Butter Pickles

8 cups sliced, unpeeled cucumbers	2 cups sugar
4 cups sliced onion	2 tablespoons mixed
¼ cup salt	pickling spices
2 cups vinegar	2 teaspoons turmeric

Place the cucumbers and the onion in a large container (*not* aluminum) and sprinkle with the salt. Allow to stand overnight, stirring occasionally. Drain thoroughly. Pour the vinegar and sugar over the vegetables and allow to stand a few hours or overnight. Put into a heavy kettle (again, *not* aluminum) and bring to a boil. Reduce heat and cook at a bare simmer for about 20 minutes. Pack into hot, sterilized jars and seal. Makes about 5 pints.

Classic pickles were allowed to stand in a very heavy brine solution for some time (old instructions tell you that the brine should be strong enough to float an egg), then rinsed, pickled, and packed into containers (or allowed to stand in covered crocks). Just in case you are having a slow month, I offer

Fourteen-Day Pickles

2 gallons cucumbers, cut in quarters	3 quarts vinegar
2 cups salt	3 quarts sugar
boiling water	pickling spice
3 tablespoons alum	

Place the cucumbers in a large glass or crockery container and cover with a brine made of the salt dissolved in 1 gallon of boiling water (or enough to cover the cucumbers). Cover the container and allow to stand for seven days. Drain. Refill with boiling water and allow to stand for 24 hours. Drain. After dissolving the alum in 1 gallon of boiling water, pour over the cucumbers and allow to stand for 24 hours. Drain. Make a syrup of the vinegar, sugar, and spices and bring to a boil. Pour over the cucumbers and allow to stand 24 hours. For each of the next four days, pour off the syrup, bring to a boil, and pour back over the cucumbers. On the fourteenth day, drain the syrup and bring it to a boil. Pack the pickles into sterilized quart jars, pour the boiling syrup over them, and seal.

I realize that every pickle recipe I have included is for a sweet pickle. As I told you, I really am not fond of any of the traditional pickles. Most people love them—there is no accounting for taste. One lone sour pickle recipe follows.

Dill Pickles

2 gallons fresh cucumbers	dill
2 cups salt	garlic
1 gallon boiling water	vinegar

Wash the cucumbers and place in a large glass or crockery container. Make a brine of the salt and the boiling water and pour over the cucumbers. Allow to stand for a week. Drain and cover the cucumbers with boiling water and allow to stand overnight. Drain. Pack the pickles into sterilized quart jars, placing a peeled clove of garlic and a head of fresh dill (or 1 teaspoon dill seed) in each quart jar. Cover with boiling vinegar and seal. Allow to stand at least 2 weeks before serving. Serve chilled.

This is probably as good a time as any to talk about relishes. In East Tennessee the classic relish is chow-chow, for which there are as many recipes as there are cooks to make it.

Chow-Chow

2 large heads of cabbage	½ cup salt
12 onions	4 tablespoons mustard seed
12 green peppers	3 tablespoons mixed
12 red sweet peppers	pickling spice
12 large green tomatoes	5 cups vinegar
1 or 2 pods hot green pepper	5 cups sugar

Coarsely grind all the vegetables (I use the coarse chopping blade on the Kitchenaid vegetable attachment). Mix the vegetables and the salt and allow to stand overnight in a glass, ceramic, or stainless steel container. Drain and squeeze out all the water possible. Tie the pickling spices in a piece of cheesecloth and place in a large kettle (*not* aluminum) with the vinegar, sugar, and mustard seed and bring to a boil. When the mixture is boiling, add the vegetables and bring back to a boil. Cook until the relish is as thick as you want it to be. Pack into hot sterilized pint jars and seal.

Cucumber relish is a nice way to use cucumbers that have gotten too large for other uses.

Cucumber Relish

6 cups large cucumbers, peeled,
 seeded, and chopped
4 large onions, chopped
4 tablespoons salt

4 tablespoons mustard seed
4 cups vinegar
4 cups sugar

Mix the cucumbers, onions, and salt and allow to stand overnight. Drain and squeeze out all the liquid possible. Add the vinegar, sugar, and mustard seed and again allow to stand overnight. Bring to a boil and cook until thick, about one hour. Pack into hot, sterilized jars and seal. This will make about a dozen half pints.

Another major summer vegetable was cabbage. Easy to grow and easy to preserve, cabbage was ideal for the summer garden. Not only was it eaten fresh all through the summer, but it could be cut and kept in any cool dark place—my great-grandparents actually had a cellar under the house where vegetables could be stored and enjoyed fresh late into the fall or early winter. When preparing cabbage, we usually fried or boiled it. Cabbage is a pleasant way to add bulk to your diet, and if you leave off the butter and add lemon juice, it is also a nice way to avoid calories.

Boiled Cabbage

1 small head of cabbage
1 cup water
3 tablespoons butter or bacon grease
salt and pepper to taste

Cut the core out of the cabbage and divide the head into quarters or large chunks. Place in a saucepan with the water and bring to a boil. Cook until the cabbage is tender. Drain, add the butter, and allow to melt. Add salt and pepper to taste. Serve hot.

Cabbage was also sometimes cooked in milk in the same way as above, but more often, it was served creamed. There were two common ways to prepare creamed cabbage. Although I prefer the one that uses fried cabbage, the other can be done with less butter. I'll give you both of them so you can decide which you like better.

Creamed Cabbage

1 small head of cabbage
1½ cups milk
2 tablespoons butter
2 tablespoons flour
salt and pepper to taste

Remove the core and cut the cabbage into large pieces. Put the cabbage and the milk into a heavy saucepan and bring to a boil. Reduce the heat and cook at a bare simmer until the cabbage is almost tender. Add the butter. Make a smooth paste of the flour and about 3 tablespoons of water and stir into the simmering cabbage. Cook, stirring constantly, until thick and smooth. Add salt to taste. Turn onto a platter and sprinkle the top with black pepper to serve. (We'll get to the other version of creamed cabbage in just a moment as a variation on fried cabbage.)

While "bile them cabbage down" may have been something to sing about, fried cabbage was eaten much more often. Generally, it was fried with pork, but sometimes with butter. Which you chose was a matter of taste and what was available. Salt-cured bacon was used often for breakfast, with any grease cooked out being carefully saved. (When hogs were killed, the fat meat was carefully rendered for lard.) This grease was the basis of a lot of cooking. For reasons of taste or availability, you will find me talking about either bacon grease or butter.

Fried Cabbage

1 small head of cabbage
3 to 4 tablespoons butter or bacon grease
1 pod of hot pepper (green, red, fresh or dried)
salt to taste

Heat the butter or grease in a heavy, cast-iron skillet with a tightly fitting lid. Add the cabbage, which has been cut into about 2-inch-square pieces. Stir to coat with the grease. Add the pepper (stem and seeds removed), cut into two or three pieces. Cover. Cook, stirring occasionally, until almost tender. Remove the cover and cook out any liquid which may have formed. Salt to taste and serve hot.

Variation: Creamed Cabbage II. Prepare fried cabbage as above, leaving out the hot pepper. When the liquid has been cooked out, add 2 tablespoons flour and stir it into the cabbage. Add 1½ cups milk and stir constantly over high heat until the mixture boils and is very thick. Add salt to taste. Turn out onto a platter and sprinkle with black pepper to serve.

Cole slaw was another of our favorite uses for cabbage.

Cole Slaw

1 small head of cabbage	3 tablespoons sugar
1 tablespoon salt	3 tablespoons vinegar
¼ cup mayonnaise	

Pare the cabbage and chop it fine (I use the coarse chopping blade on the Kitchenaid vegetable chopper attachment for the mixer or the coarse chopping disk on the Cuisinart.) Add the salt and allow to stand at room temperature for at least ½ hour. Pour the cabbage into a linen dish towel and squeeze it as dry as possible. Put it back in the bowl, add the mayonnaise, sugar, and vinegar, and mix thoroughly. Chill at least a couple of hours before serving. If you like, you can add chopped onion, carrot, or green pepper to the cabbage.

Perhaps the most interesting reason for growing cabbage was to make kraut. This almost universally known method of preserving not only cabbage but a whole range of other vegetables depends upon adding salt and sometimes other spices to the vegetables, packing them tightly into containers, and allowing them to ferment in a more or less controlled way. Traditional East Tennessee kraut was particularly simple to make. Cabbage was chopped or shredded fine, mixed with salt, packed into crocks or jars, and allowed to ferment. If the kraut was packed into jars, the fermentation was slowed by sealing the jars after a few days, and the kraut would keep for months.

Making kraut is something you might enjoy trying. It has a slightly different taste from commercial kraut, and I like it much better. Prepare it one summer so you can be ready for backbones and ribs next winter. I know no way to give a precise recipe for kraut. I will instead give you the method, and you can simply adapt it to whatever amount of cabbage you happen to have.

To make **kraut,** shred or chop the cabbage fine. (For chopped kraut, I have found that the Kitchenaid chopper works very well.) Mix about 3 tablespoons of salt for each ½ gallon of chopped cabbage. The cabbage should have a decidedly salty taste. Loosely fill a quart jar with the cabbage. Then, using something which will fit down into the neck of the jar, pack the cabbage just as firmly as possible into the jar. You cannot overpack. If the cabbage is too loose, it will turn dark and spoil. Continue to add cabbage and to pack until the jar is tightly filled up to the start of the threads. Close the jar with a scalded rubber jar ring and a zinc lid. (These can still be found in the canning sections of some grocery or hardware stores.) Turn the lid on tight and then loosen half a turn. Continue packing until all the cabbage has been used.

You will have generated a considerable amount of excess liquid; if you wish, you can put it in quart jars and seal them in the same way to make kraut juice. (Pouring it out is also an option.) Place the filled jars in a cool, dark place on several layers of newspaper—maybe in the garage or somewhere outside the house. Over the next two weeks, the cabbage will ferment and the jars will overflow. The fermentation produces a fairly strong, yeasty smell which tends to permeate things. (If a neighbor asks if you have a run of mash going, ask him how he knows the smell.)

At the end of two weeks, this process should have stopped. Carefully wipe the outsides of the jars with a damp cloth and tighten the lids as tightly as possible. Continue to store in a cool, dark place. Kraut will keep for several months.

If you are really filled with the pioneer spirit, you can try making kraut the way my mother's family did for years. Use the same method as above, but instead of packing the cabbage into jars, pack it into an earthenware crock. When you have packed all the cabbage into the crock, cover the top completely with two or three layers of the large leaves you have reserved from the outside of the cabbage. Cover the cabbage with a clean white cloth and place on it a wooden cover which you have cut to fit over the cloth. Place a weight on the wooden cover (a clean rock works fine) and allow the cabbage to stand at least a month before starting to use it. To use, simply remove all the covering, take out what you want, and recover the rest.

My Grandpa Weaver had cut a small white oak maul which he kept just for packing kraut. My mother still has a piece of an oak limb which has been smoothed on one end to form a handle which she uses to pack kraut into jars. As for me, I use the wooden pusher which came with the Kitchenaid meat grinder. I'm sure you can find something.

Kraut-making was another of those communal activities which were so much a part of country life. As a small child, I can remember seeing a table of boards set up on sawhorses in the yard at the Weavers' to make kraut. The women would chop the cabbage and place it into large dishpans where it was salted. Grandpa Weaver would then sit down with the large kraut crocks on the ground and proceed to pack the cabbage very tightly, cover it with cabbage leaves, and place it in the cellar or the smoke-house to ferment. Everyone was involved in producing something for everyone to enjoy.

A first cousin of kraut is something which I had only seen done in my family. These little delicacies are called "Mangoes," and I have no idea why. They certainly do not relate to the semi-tropical fruit of the same name in any way at all. They are a little trouble to make but do make an interesting addition to a relish tray. It's not likely that you will run into anyone else bringing them to the church social. (Recently, though, I actually came across another recipe for mangoes! It was in a cookbook dating from 1913: Martha McCulloch-Williams' *Dishes & Beverages of the Old South*. Her recipe is similar to the one here but uses green peppers or young, small melons instead of green tomatoes.)

Mangoes

green tomatoes   vinegar
cabbage prepared for kraut   water

Cut one slice off the stem end of each tomato and leave the slice whole to use as a lid. Hollow out the tomatoes, discard the seeds and chop the pulp finely and mix with enough salted cabbage which has been prepared for kraut to fill each of the tomatoes. Replace the tops on the tomatoes and tie into place with white sewing thread. Pack the tomatoes into wide-mouthed jars just large enough to hold them and be full. Heat sufficient cider vinegar mixed half with water to cover the tomatoes. Bring the vinegar and water mixture to a boil, and pour it over the tomatoes. Cover tightly and then loosen the lids half a turn. Place the jars in a cool, dark place on several layers of newspaper. Allow to ferment for two weeks. Wipe off any material which has overflowed and tighten the lids. Store in a cool, dark place. Mangoes will keep several months but will start to lose their flavor if stored too long. They are good served chilled.

We commonly grew two kinds of squash in the summer. The yellow crooknecked **summer squash** was grown to fry with onions. Simply cut tender, young squash crosswise and fry it with chopped onions in bacon grease. When it has almost finished cooking, add salt and pepper to taste. I'm sorry to offend the nutritionists again, but this dish was cooked until the squash was very soft and most of the liquid had cooked out.

We also grew a number of varieties of **sweet, hard-shelled squash,** including butternut, acorn, and sweet potato squash. These were all cooked in basically the same ways. One method was to cut the squash out of the shell, cut it up into small squares, and parboil it, then bake it in an ovenproof dish with butter and sugar (sometimes sprinkled with nutmeg). A more popular way of cooking them was to cut the squash in half lengthwise and to remove the seeds and the seed membrane. The seed cavity was then filled with butter and brown sugar and sprinkled with nutmeg. They were then placed in a shallow pan with a very small amount of water and baked in a 350° oven until they were tender and lightly browned. They could be served either warm or cold.

I suppose I should really confess about one practice I'm following in all these recipes. I regularly give you precise oven temperatures as if we cooked that way. We did not. In the first place, we are talking about cooking on a wood-burning stove. Temperature was at best a chancy matter. If you wanted something to cook fast, you set it near the firebox. If you wanted it to simmer, you put it further down the stove, away from the fire and near where the kettle of water stayed on the stove all the time. The oven had a temperature gauge which gave you precise information like cool, warm, and hot—if the gauge still worked at all. I have seen country women regularly check the oven temperature by simply holding their hand into the oven for a few seconds. Precise this is not.

Mammy Dossett was a true believer in wood stoves. She lived out her life in the house where I was born—in the last years, however, it took considerable efforts by her daughters to make it possible. Although in her later years she had first a kerosene stove and then an electric one in her big kitchen, she never gave up the wood-burning stove and would fire it up summer or winter if she wanted to cook something special. She was convinced that food tasted better cooked on a wood burning stove, and who am I to argue?

Fairness demands that I tell you in advance what I've been telling other folks for years—that there are only two foods that I really do not care for. One is buttermilk to drink (it's great to cook with, but the texture is intolerable for a beverage); the other is blackberries. In truth, I probably do like blackberries, but by now I've told the story of why I don't so many times that I am now convinced that it is true.

When I was growing up, I hated picking blackberries. My mother, however, believed the activity to be the greatest thing in the whole world. That meant I had to devote the entire month of July to finding ways to keep from doing it. The struggle was monumental, but she always won. I once decided that the easy way to avoid picking berries was simply to agree to do so and then not. I went into the pasture, where the briers grew in profusion, found a nice tree, lay down in the shade, and went to sleep. For the next week I did not have to pick berries because I was so covered with chiggers that I could not walk. In case you don't know, chiggers are a variety of microscopic spiders which burrow under the skin to lay their eggs and die. They itch, burn, sting, swell, and do various other things which produce an almost uncontrollable urge to remove your skin. They also tend to accumulate at the points where clothing fits tightly. I probably don't need to give you any further explanation of what this means, but I will tell you that I couldn't wear pants for a week. And with that, I certainly don't need to tell you why I remember that time whenever I think of blackberries!

For those normal folks who didn't seem to mind briers, chiggers, snakes, sunburn, and various other hardships you had to endure to secure them, blackberries were always available. They grew wild in pasture fields, fencerows and almost everywhere else. That brier patch which Br'er Rabbit feared so much was a blackberry patch. They were made into pies and dumplings, jams and jellies. They were canned to have something sweet in the winter. It would be un-Tennessean not to revere them. Therefore, for my wife and all others who love them, here are some blackberry recipes.

Blackberry Cobbler

pie crust for an 8-inch pan (see p. 175)
3 cups blackberries
¾ cup sugar
4 tablespoons butter

Line an 8-inch-square baking dish with pie crust, allowing extra crust to hang over the sides rather than cutting it off. Bring the berries and sugar slowly to a boil in a heavy saucepan. Do not add water. Juice will form as the berries get hot. Pour the hot berries into the pie shell. Dot the top of the berries with small pieces of butter. Fold the edges of the crust over into the berries. Use scraps of dough to fill in open spaces in the center of the pie. Bake in a 350° oven about 30 minutes or until brown.

Quick Blackberry Cobbler

½ cup all purpose flour

½ cup sugar

½ cup milk

2 teaspoons baking powder

¼ cup butter

3 cups blackberries cooked

   with ¾ cup sugar

Melt the butter in an 8-inch-square cobbler pan. Mix together the flour, baking powder, and sugar. Stir in the milk to make a thick batter. Pour the batter into the pan with the butter, then pour the hot berries over the batter. Bake in a 350° oven about 30 minutes or until brown. These instructions are correct. It will look like a mess, but the berries settle through the batter as it rises to the top to make a very good cobbler.

A major reason for picking blackberries is for jam and jelly. (I must admit a great fondness for blackberry jam cake with caramel icing. Without the jam you cannot have the cake.) A word about blackberry jelly. Blackberries are not strong in pectin, the substance which causes jelly to jell. For this reason, apple juice was sometimes added to the blackberry juice to be sure to have a good jelly. Sometimes apple peels were simply cooked with blackberries which were to be used for jam and jelly, and it aided the jelling of both. With jam it really doesn't matter. With jelly, though, a proper jell is important. My mother tells me that I overemphasize this problem, but I can recall jelly that didn't shake but ran.

Blackberry Jelly and Jam

blackberries

apple juice (if desired)

sugar

Cook whatever amount of berries you have available. Pour the cooked berries into a colander which has been lined with several thicknesses of cheesecloth, or use a jelly bag. Allow as much of the juice to run through as will without squeezing the bag. Reserve the berries for the jam. Measure the juice and if you wish add about 1 cup of apple juice for each 3 or 4 cups of blackberry juice. Add 1 cup of sugar for each cup of the combined juices. Bring to a boil. Reduce heat but continue to maintain at a hard boil, stirring occasionally and keeping any foam that forms skimmed off. Boil until the mixture reaches 220° on a candy thermometer or until a small amount of the jelly placed on a cold saucer jells immediately. Pour the jelly into hot, dry, thoroughly sterilized jars and seal with paraffin or a sealing lid.

For **blackberry jam,** use the cooked berries reserved above and press the berries through a colander or a medium sieve to remove the seeds. Measure the berries and add an equal amount of sugar. Put the mixture in a heavy pan and bring to a boil, stirring constantly. Reduce the heat and continue to boil the mixture, stirring occasionally, until it is thick and a small amount placed on a cold saucer becomes firm. Pour into hot, dry, thoroughly sterilized jars and seal with paraffin or sealing lids.

Some folks now cook jam or fruit butters in the oven. If you prefer that method, place the fruit and sugar into a flat pan and cook in a 350° oven, stirring occasionally until thick. Can as above.

Summertime was also the time for the all-day dinner and singing on the grounds we talked about earlier. These "meetings" could take several forms. Perhaps the most usual—which I am happy to report is still alive in many rural churches—was the "homecoming," which was just what the name implies. It was a day set aside for all those folks who had gone off into the city—

whether Knoxville or Detroit—to come back and partake of their heritage. There would be preaching, singing, and eating. There would be lots of visiting and gossiping and maybe some more singing and almost surely some more eating. All this could very easily last all day.

Sometimes such an event might be on a Saturday rather than a Sunday and be devoted to doing whatever work was needed at the church. A country church did not hire someone to repair the roof or fix a window in the church. It was understood that a part of being a member of the church meant being able to give time to get those things done. If everyone got together, it was possible to accomplish a great deal while having a wonderful time. It also meant that lunch could be a part of what you did.

I have mentioned earlier that Grandpa and Granny Weaver were devoted Methodists. They and all their family were members of Clapps Chapel Methodist Church. Since they never had much money, Grandpa always felt an especially strong need to work at the church, particularly donating time to help with its upkeep. He and Granny are now buried in the cemetery of that church, just as they wanted.

While you might not find it at all that interesting to talk about the necessity of maintaining the common ground of country cemeteries and filling graves that had sunk, or helping a neighbor right a tombstone which had fallen, or painting a church in a single afternoon, I think you will enjoy hearing about the food. I don't want to imply by anything I say that I believe that the good Christian women of any East Tennessee rural church could possibly have been competitive in preparing food. But it does seem to my imperfect memory that some of the best food I ever had was at those dinners. I suppose it was pure coincidence that the best green beans, sliced tomatoes, potato salad, baked squash, custard pies, lemon pies and, of course, fried chicken were spread on those big tables (which were really just boards put on saw horses) and covered with a patchwork of the best tablecloths from all the families in the church. Homemade light bread, biscuits and corn-bread and, of course, cakes—apple stack cake, blackberry jam cake, pound cake—all competed for the attention of the people who came. Sometimes when you really wanted to show off a little, you might even take banana pudding, but that could be viewed as a little too much. I don't think that St. Paul had a lot to say about food, but there might have been another letter if he had made it to one of those events.

Some things are easy to lose sight of in today's world. We are talking about church picnics and about to talk about fried chicken, clearly the most important single food at such events. Today, the season of the year has little to do with what you can and cannot do. In the old days, however, country church dinners were held in the summertime because they had to be held outside. (I first encountered church dining rooms and recreation rooms during my high school years, and that was in a church in Knoxville, not Corryton.) Likewise, fried chicken was a summer dish because that is when you had chickens for frying.

In the spring, hens will follow their built-in timetable and begin to make a nest where they will "set" and incubate their eggs. A good "setting hen" will welcome other eggs placed under her. She will also defend the nest vigorously and will attack any-one, including a small, curious boy, who happens to come close. When these chicks hatch, they are raised in the barnyard by the

hen. At about 8 to 12 weeks, those chicks are ready to fry, especially the roosters. Given a few more weeks, they will have gone past the stage when they are tender enough to fry and start to become either a part of the egg-laying stock or the chicken stock. You understand, we are not talking about chickens whose dainty feet never touch the ground and who eat only cracked corn with certain antibiotics added. When you scratch in the barnyard with the big boys, you tend to grow up fast.

Neither are we talking about chickens which arrive in the kitchen in neat plastic packages. When I was growing up, chickens got to the kitchen only if somebody went to the yard, caught them, killed them, cleaned them, cut them up, washed them, and then brought them to the skillet. My Mammy Dossett still holds the world's record for the dispatching of chickens. She would walk through the chicken yard until she saw exactly the young rooster she was interested in. A little chicken feed on the ground would distract the unsuspecting victim until she could get close. Then with one quick grab, she would firmly grasp the bird by the neck and, with one firm twist, separate head from chicken. Stepping daintily aside while that particular bird flapped its last flap, she then waited until the excitement died down and moved on to the next participant in that day's dinner.

Somehow, remembering the fact that Mammy was able to wring the head off a chicken brings to mind an interesting facet of her personality. Although she revered my late grandfather and spoke of him in hushed tones, she did not have the same feelings for his family. She was given to saying that all Lamberts must be related because after the Lord saw the first set, He certainly wouldn't have made any more. One of her favorite tales was about some relative of my grandfather's who couldn't wring a chicken's neck and had to use an axe instead. One day, the unfortunate fellow cut off not only the chicken's head but also one of his fingers. When his father came in from the fields that night, he asked how the accident happened. In demonstrating, the boy cut off another finger. (You may judge for yourself the veracity of this story.)

Now this is as good a time as any to let you in on another of my deep-seated prejudices. Remember how I feel about cows? Compared to how I feel about chickens, I absolutely love cows. As far as I am concerned, the only good chicken is one cooked just to taste. But in spite of being ugly, dirty, and—most of all—stupid, they were an integral, inescapable part of farm life.

I suppose it is now safe to tell one misadventure from my youth which I have hitherto suppressed. When I was a teenager, and therefore bitterly opposed to doing anything worthwhile, my tasks included feeding the chickens. My father had somewhere acquired a number of boxes of stale breakfast cereal, which we then fed to the chickens.

Being resourceful by nature, I discovered that the task of opening the boxes and scattering the cereal could be accomplished in a pleasant way by throwing the boxes into the air and taking my best baseball swing at them with a tobacco stick as they fell. The box split open and flew through the air, scattering cornflakes everywhere. It was a teenage dream that I was getting better at it all the time.

Unfortunately, my physical dexterity has never equaled my resourcefulness. On one particularly good pitch, I swung and missed. Lightning quick, I saw that the box was still in the air and swung back in the other direction with great force. Somehow I failed to notice that a large hen was between the stick and the box. The tobacco stick struck that large hen squarely in her thin neck and separated her head from her body.

By this time in my life, I was about six feet tall and probably weighed about two hundred pounds. My mother stood about five feet four and may have weighed a hundred and twenty. I was not about to tell so formidable a foe that I had just decapitated one of her fat red hens while playing at feeding the chickens. So I did the only conceivable thing. I held a quiet funeral for that hen and buried her in the loose dirt near the barn. And for more than thirty years, I kept my mouth shut. I may be a coward, but I'm not stupid.

You do not need details on how to scald, pluck, singe, gut, and cut up a chicken. In today's world our food is neatly separated from the getting of it, and I'm glad it's that way. But I think that we ought to remember that as recently as forty years ago, cleaning your own chickens was the norm and not the exception. I'm not foolish enough to advocate a return to this way of life; and I maintain wholeheartedly that if you see me back on the farm, I have been faced with the choice of going back or starving. At the same time, I'm not at all sure that progress demands that we now buy chicken in little unrecognizable hunks and do nothing for ourselves.

Since there are almost as many ways to fry chicken as there are cooks—and ardent admirers of each of the ways—I can just scratch the surface with the few recipes I have room for here. One general technique I was taught (and many people still swear by it) was to cut up the chicken the night before and let it stand overnight in a bowl of salt water in the refrigerator; this gives the meat a lighter color. I've never been absolutely sure that it was worth the effort, but I still do it most of the time.

Traditional Fried Chicken

1 frying chicken (3 to 4 pounds) cut up	black pepper
½ cup flour	grease for frying
1 teaspoon salt	

Mix the salt and pepper with the flour. Dry the pieces of chicken and roll in the flour to coat the pieces on all sides. (Or simply place the flour, salt, and pepper in a plastic bag with the chicken and shake gently to coat.) Heat lard, solid shortening, or cooking oil about ¼ inch deep in a cast-iron skillet (preferably one with a good cover) until hot. Place the chicken in the hot fat in a single layer. Reduce the heat slightly but keep the grease very hot. Cover. Turn the chicken at regular intervals until it is browned on all sides and cooked through. This should take about 30 minutes. If your skillet will not hold all the pieces in a single layer, repeat the process until all pieces of chicken are cooked. Drain. Fried chicken can be served hot, room temperature, or even cold if any lasts that long.

Variations. If you like a heavier crust, dip the chicken first in the flour, salt and pepper mixture, then in a batter made of an egg beaten into a cup of milk, and finally back into the flour before frying. To get a crisp batter, it helps to put the grease about ½ inch deep in the pan and not cover the pan.

If you like a really heavy crust, dip the chicken in buttermilk and then roll in flour and fry as above.

If you like crusts *really* crunchy, make a batter of an egg, ½ cup of flour, ¼ cup cornstarch, 1 teaspoon salt and enough water to make the mixture about the consistency of thick cream. Dip each piece of the chicken into this batter and deep fry it. (This is really a Chinese batter, but it makes great chicken. In fact, boneless chicken cooked this way and dipped into a mixture of coarse ground salt and ground Szechuan peppercorns is a wonderful cocktail treat.)

Although I hadn't planned to talk about it yet, I find I can't talk about fried chicken without talking about milk gravy. They may not be completely inseparable, but they come very close. Sunday dinner in the summer was not complete without fried chicken, milk gravy, mashed potatoes, biscuits, green beans, sliced tomatoes, fried okra, baked . . . I'm sorry, I lost it there for a minute, but you get the idea.

I wish I could tell you exactly how to make milk gravy that will always be smooth, delicious, and exactly right, but I cannot. I'll tell you most of what I know and then wish you luck. Although I've been trying my hand at this only about forty years, I don't really have it perfect yet. I will tell you this: If gravy thickens immediately when it boils, you have too much flour. If it never gets thick, then you have too little. If, after you've boiled it for two or three minutes, stirring for all you're worth, it becomes thick and smooth and starts "making nickels and dimes," you have it made. Ma Freeman taught me that, and so I know it is true. If you don't know exactly what "making nickels and dimes" means, stick with me a while and I'll try to explain.

Milk Gravy

6 tablespoons grease in which chicken was fried	4 cups milk
	salt and pepper to taste
6 tablespoons flour	

Drain the grease from the pan in which chicken has been fried and return 6 tablespoons of it to the skillet. Heat the grease until fairly hot and stir in the flour. Stir constantly and allow the flour to cook and start to brown. Stir in all the milk. Continue to cook over medium-high heat, stirring constantly. Be sure to stir along the bottom of the pan constantly to loosen any brown bits from the chicken which are sticking there and to prevent the gravy from sticking. Continue to cook and stir until the gravy boils and starts to form both large and small bubbles ("nickels and dimes") on the surface, indicating that it is thick enough. Serve hot.

Milk gravy, a standard feature in country cooking, can be made in the pan where any kind of meat—pork chops, chicken, even salt bacon—has been fried. We'll talk more about chicken and milk gravy and biscuits and cornbread and all that later. However, with all this talk about canning and plowing and other chores, we ought to stop and rest a minute. In fact, I'm afraid that I haven't given enough time to the all-important subject of what you did to rest from these labors.

First, it wasn't necessary to be doing something to be resting. No TV was necessary (no TV was available), and no radio was necessary (you listened to it only in the early evenings and then only sometimes). What you did was sit. If the shade was hitting the front porch, you might sit in the swing and swing lazily back and forth. There were some disadvantages to swinging. If you happened to be hiding out from tasks which needed doing, the faint squeak of the swing chains would give you away every time. "Get out of that swing and get that yard mowed, boy," someone would say. If the sun was on the porch, you would sit beside the house in the big old wooden lawn chairs or the new metal ones (which have suddenly come back into vogue). You might possibly drink lemonade, but you probably just sat there. You might fan with an old paper fan that you had been given by some funeral home and you might talk, or if you were the favored grandson, you might get someone to read to you from one of your two or three prized books. If someone had come through selling watermelon off a truck, you might even have watermelon which you had cooled in the springhouse. But you might just sit in the cool of the evening and listen to the crickets and the whip-poor-will off in the distance.

While they were "settin'," the men might be following one of the important rituals of this part of the country: whittling. I once asked Grandpa Weaver what he was making as he sat carefully whittling down a piece of red cedar. Without looking up, he said, "Shavings." And there you have the essence of East Tennessee whittling. A man just sat with a small piece of wood and a small knife and drew the knife down along the piece of wood, making a thin, curly shaving. The piece of wood would be absolutely smooth and round and useless. When you had finished one session of whittling (God only knows how you knew when you had finished), you would fold up your penknife, put it back into your pocket, and tuck the piece of wood away somewhere until the next time. I suppose that things were just simpler then.

Right now though, we can't just be sitting here. There are tomatoes to can and beans to dry and blackberries to pick and can and make into jelly and jam, and there are preserves to make, and I don't really have time to talk anymore. Come back next chapter and we'll have more time.

4
Fall

For the sake of argument, let's have fall begin on Labor Day. I know that that's not really when fall begins, but remember, all the divisions in this book are arbitrary anyway. I'm not really sure that any clear distinction between the end of summer and the beginning of fall can be made or would mean anything if it were. I do know that work for the winter, in the best tradition of the industrious ant, carried right through until about Thanksgiving. Actually, I picked Labor Day because that is about when the good fall apples start to be available.

Apple and pear trees appeared on almost every farm. Some people had peach trees as well. Plums were also common. A lot of people had grapevines—usually thick-hulled Concord grapes —and loved to hunt wild muscadines or scuppernong grapes in the summer and fall. These fruits, along with blackberries, dewberries and strawberries, which we talked about back in "Spring" and "Summer," were the mainstays for desserts. Pies made from fresh fruit or from canned fruit were usual. So were jelly, jam, and preserves.

At both the Dossetts' and the Weavers', there were apple and pear trees. The varieties of apple trees had been selected so that some kind of apples was available every season. I've already told you about early transparents. Later came Rustycoats and Grimes Golden and Winesaps. Mammy Dossett also had one tree of Stark Delicious apples for "eating" apples and for a special use we will talk more about later. The pears were the big, old, hard ones she called "horse pears" (no doubt because only a horse could munch them raw). The pear trees were in an orchard some little distance from the house and planted in neat rows.

Like many other East Tennessee farmers, we also had plum trees scattered around the house yard. Recently, when I visited the place of my birth, the only things I found remaining were a couple of plum trees that my father and I had planted before I was seven.

At the Weavers', a big section of the back yard was devoted to grapevines, which hung full of purple Concord grapes in the late summer. Grapes were eaten fresh, made into grape juice or grape preserves, or made into grape pies. I now discover that grape pie is something of a mystery to most people. I have seen it served in a restaurant only once—at the wonderful Satsuma Tearoom in Nashville. (If you haven't had lunch at the Satsuma, then you've never really known Nashville. By the way, this restaurant, founded in about 1920, serves dinner only one night each year. That night is the annual Christmas dinner, in early December. It is well worth planning to be in Nashville for it, even though you will probably have to stand in a two-block-long line to get in.)

Grape Cobbler

4 cups uncooked Concord grapes
¾ cup sugar
crust for an 8-inch
    cobbler (see p. 175)

crust for an 8-inch
    cobbler (see p. 175)

Pop the center out of the grapes into one saucepan and place the hulls in another. Add the sugar to the hulls and bring each of the mixtures to a slow boil. Do not add water to either. Simply heat the mixtures slowly, and juice will form. Boil each about 5 minutes or until the centers of the grapes start to break up and the seeds to loosen. Run the center through a colander or strainer to remove the seeds. Stir thoroughly to ensure that as much of the pulp as possible goes through. Combine the grape pulp with the cooked hulls. Line an 8-inch cobbler pan with the dough, and pour the grape mixture into it. Fold over the edges and cover the top with dough. Sprinkle the top with sugar. Bake in a 350° oven about 35 minutes or until brown.

Variation. For a grape pie with a double pastry crust (see p. 175), the filling is made the same way except some kind of thickener is added. A couple of tablespoons of small tapioca will do that nicely, as will an equal amount of cornstarch or even flour.

Now let's get back to apples. A number of varieties grow well in this area, and substantial commercial apple orchards have been operating near Cosby in the foothills of the Smokies for a couple of generations now. Both sour apples for cooking and sweet apples for eating are grown. I like a sour apple or a good general purpose apple like the Winesap or the Jonathan best both for cooking and eating. I have little interest in an apple that is not crisp and not at least slightly tart.

"As American as apple pie" has a clear meaning for me. Until we moved into Knoxville when I was seventeen, we always had an orchard, which meant we always had apples. When we lived at my grandmother's home, I can remember her making apple butter in a huge kettle which was hung over an outside fire. She even had a specially made paddle with a long handle which allowed you to stir the cooking apple butter constantly without getting too near the fire. Apple pie or apple cobbler were a part of our everyday diet. At least two ways of making apple dumplings were common, and both were good. Apples were eaten raw, cooked, canned, and dried—and kept in straw in the cellar so they would last until Christmas.

By now you may have guessed that my relationship with Mammy Dossett's second husband was a strange one. Although they had been married years before I was born, it was always made clear to me that he was not my grandfather. I heard all sorts of encomiums on that legendary figure from my grandmother and by my aunts. Dad Dossett was a nice man who somehow always existed just at the edge of my consciousness even when I lived in what was, in fact, his house. You have also noticed by now that I have always referred to it as Mammy Dossett's house. Perhaps the Freudians among you can explain how this man could have been so much a part of my life and seem as unimportant as he does. I don't know. But there it is. Anyway, the point of this story was supposed to be that apple pie was even a part of our folklore: One of the few things I remember strongly about Dad Dossett was his reciting a long bit of doggerel which began "A Apple Pie" and proceeded through the alphabet about that pie. I remember that "B baked it, C cut it, D divided it, E eat it, F fought for it, G got it, H had it, I eyed it, . . . (don't blame me—I'm just remembering!) right on through all the letters.

Beyond all this, apple pie is one of those tastes that is as easy to get today as it was forty years ago when I was a child. If you happen to live in East Tennessee and you want to have an apple experience of the highest order, drive some Sunday to have lunch at the Log Cabin Inn at Cosby, and then, after lunch, visit one of the apple orchards that line the road on the way to Gatlinburg and select a bushel of apples of your choice or buy a peck each of several kinds and try out these recipes. If that doesn't help you recapture a part of your heritage, you are probably beyond hope (and perhaps are some sort of subversive). Of course, while I was living in New England I discovered that those folks believe the apples up there are just as good as we think ours are here in the mountains of East Tennessee. My greatest fear is that they may be right. Whoever is right, here is a basic apple pie, with a couple of its many variations.

Basic Apple Pie

6 to 8 cooking apples (Winesap, Jonathan, Wolf River, Granny Smith)

¾ cup sugar

2 tablespoons all-purpose flour

4 tablespoons butter

1 tablespoon cinnamon

pastry for a 2-crust pie (see p. 175)

Peel, core, and slice the apples into thin slices. Line a 9-inch pie pan with the pastry and fill it with the uncooked apple slices. Mix the sugar, flour, and cinnamon together and spread over the apples. Dot the top of the pie with the butter. Cover with pastry, sealing the edges carefully. Make slits in the top of the pastry in a pleasing pattern to allow the steam to escape. Bake about 1 hour in a 325° oven. Cover the edges of the pie with thin strips of foil if they start to brown too much. Serve warm.

Variations:

(1) Prepare the pie as above except to mix together the apples and the flour, sugar, and cinnamon mixture before you put it into the bottom crust. Dot with the butter and then cover the top with a lattice made of pastry cut into ¾-inch strips.

(2) Prepare the pie as above except to add ¼ cup freshly squeezed orange juice before putting on the top crust. The top of an apple pie (or any other double crust pie) will glaze nicely if you brush the top with water and sprinkle it lightly with sugar just when it starts to brown.

Crumb Top Apple Pie

6 to 8 tart apples

½ cup sugar

cinnamon

pastry for a 1-crust pie (see p. 175)

crumb topping

Peel, core, and slice the apples thinly and place in an 8- or 9-inch pie pan lined with pastry. Sprinkle with the sugar and shake the pie to distribute the sugar down into the apples. Sprinkle with cinnamon. Cover with a crumb topping made of ¼ cup sugar and ½ cup all-purpose flour with 6 tablespoons cold butter worked into it. Bake in a 350° oven about 45 minutes or until brown on the top.

Apple Cobbler

3 cups cooked apples, unsweetened   cinnamon

¾ cup sugar   pie crust for an 8-inch

4 tablespoons butter   cobbler pan (see p. 175)

Line an 8-inch cobbler pan with pie dough, allowing the dough to hang over the edge. Pour the cooked apples into the dough and sprinkle with the sugar and the cinnamon. Dot with the butter. Fold the dough over onto the apples and fill the center with small strips of dough if necessary. Bake at 350° for 30 minutes or until the top is brown.

Some time ago, I promised you apple dumplings and then got distracted by apple pie. Here are the two varieties I was talking about.

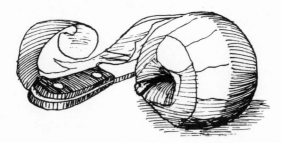

Baked Apple Dumplings

6 tart apples, peeled, cored, and left whole   sugar

1 recipe of either pie crust or pastry (see p. 175)   butter

                                                      cinnamon

Roll the pie dough or pastry thin. Cut into squares large enough to enclose the apples completely. Place an apple in the middle of each square. Fill the opening where the core was removed with butter, sugar, and cinnamon. Completely enclose the apple in the pastry and seal it closed. Place in a shallow baking pan and put a small amount of water in the pan. Bake in a 350° oven about 45 minutes or until brown. Serve warm with fresh cream.

Boiled Apple Dumplings

6 or 8 tart apples, peeled,
   cored, and sliced
1 cup sugar
1 quart water

½ teaspoon cinnamon
a pinch of salt
dumpling dough (see p. 28)

Mix the apples, sugar, and water and bring to a boil. Allow the apples to cook until almost done. Drop the dumplings into the boiling juice and cook until done. Add the pinch of salt and the cinnamon. Serve warm with cream.

Apples—cooked or in applesauce—were a regular part of breakfast almost year-round. For **cooked apples,** simply peel, core, and chop them and cook in a heavy saucepan with sugar to taste. **Applesauce** is almost as easy. Without peeling the apples, cut them into quarters and remove the core. Add a small amount of water and cook until tender. Run the apples through a colander to remove the peels and add sugar to taste. If the applesauce seems too thin, simply boil it slowly until it reaches the desired consistency. Applesauce can't be too thick—that's a rule. The next logical step is

Apple Butter

Mix unsweetened applesauce and sugar in the proportion of about 4 cups applesauce to about 3 cups sugar. If the apples are very sour, you may want to use equal portions. The amount makes no difference at all. Anything from one cup to one barrel works equally well. For each quart of apple and sugar mixture, add one cinnamon stick about 3 or 4 inches long. Bring slowly to a full boil, then reduce the heat to the lowest level which will maintain a steady boil. Cook, stirring almost constantly, until thick enough that a small amount of the mixture will jell on a cold saucer. Pour into hot, sterilized jars and seal.

Creditable apple butter can also be made by following the procedure above except putting the apple-sugar-cinnamon mixture into a 350° oven in a flat pan and allowing it to cook down while stirring it occasionally.

A couple of tips about apple butter and jams and jellies in general. Some folks make apple butter by grinding cored apples with the peel on and boiling the mixture down with sugar. Others do not cook the apple butter down enough to jell but prefer it much thinner. I understand that an interesting apple butter can be made by reducing the sugar slightly and using cinnamon red hot candies instead of the cinnamon sticks. Variations like that are a matter of taste. I've described what I prefer, but you shouldn't hesitate to experiment. If you believe that cooking is a science rather than an art and want everything in precise measure and exact procedure, you are reading the wrong book. (But you have a right to cook that way if you want to. The right to be wrong is to be defended to the death if necessary.)

Since the subject of canning has come up again, I'll again remind you that home-canned foods need to be processed in a pressure cooker or a water-bath canner if they are to be safe to use. The current feeling is that *everything*—even jams, jellies, pickles, and relishes—should be processed. Fine. I advise you to do so for your own safety. I do know that back when I was growing up the rate of loss of the low-acid foods was high. I also know that jams, jellies, preserves and pickles were not traditionally processed that way. The material that I have read recently says that these easy-to-preserve foods, after they are sealed, should be processed in a water bath for 5 minutes. Check a good book on canning for the best means of doing the water-bath process-ing. So there—you have both the traditional and the best modern thinking.

Apple jelly is very good. It can also be the basis for a whole range of other flavored jellies. The only one of these that was traditionally done was mint jelly. But for those of you who enjoy the flavor of herbs and like jelly as an accompaniment to roast meat, I offer some variations.

Apple Jelly

apple juice

sugar

Use about 3 cups of sugar for each 4 cups of apple juice. Again the proportion is important, the amount is not. Bring to a full boil and cook to 220° on a candy thermometer or until a couple of drops on a cold saucer jells. Pour into hot, dry, sterilized jars and seal.

Mint Jelly. Place one cup of fresh mint, thoroughly washed, in a heavy saucepan with one quart of water. Bring to a boil and remove from the heat. Cover and allow to steep for at least an hour. Strain and add the liquid to 2 quarts of apple juice. Proceed to make apple jelly as described above. You may add a little green food color just before canning the jelly if you like.

Sweet Basil Jelly. Proceed exactly as for mint jelly except use ½ cup fresh sweet basil rather than the mint.

Thyme Jelly. Proceed as for mint jelly except use ¼ cup fresh thyme instead of the mint. This recipe is particularly good if you use lemon thyme. (What do you mean, Where do you get lemon thyme? You grow it in a flower bed, of course!)

When I was growing up, apple juice for apple jelly was often gotten by boiling the apple peels with water almost to cover and then straining the juice through a jelly cloth. There was also another way to make apple jelly and apple butter. The apples were cut up and placed in a pot with about half as much water as fruit and cooked until very tender. Then the juice was drained off and strained through a jelly cloth to make jelly and the pulp was run through a colander for the apple butter. Waste not, want not!

An interesting use of apples which I have never encountered except in my family and which I have never found in any cookbook is apple preserves. They are a fair amount of trouble, and I don't think you will want to do a lot of them, but they are an interesting novelty. My city-raised wife thinks they are wonderful on vanilla ice cream, and who am I to argue with a person of such refined tastes? Apple preserves were the reason we had the Stark Delicious apples which I talked about earlier. They must be made with apples which will not cook up, and the Stark Delicious or the Washington Delicious fits this requirement. If you are buying these in the store, be sure they are still very firm. If they are too ripe, they will fall apart, and you will have gone to a lot of trouble for nothing.

Apple Preserves

8 cups Red Delicious apples

6 cups sugar

3 tablespoons mixed pickling spices (or whole cloves)

Peel the apples, core them, and slice into thin slices. Place the apple slices and the sugar in a glass, ceramic, or stainless steel container, cover, and refrigerate overnight. The sugar should dissolve and a considerable amount of juice form. Put the apples and the juice in a pan (*not* aluminum) and place on the burner. Tie the spices (from which you have picked any dried red pepper) into a square of cheesecloth, and drop it into the apples. Bring to a full boil and reduce the heat just enough to keep the mixture at a boil. Cook until the syrup becomes very thick, and a small amount of it placed on a cold saucer jells right away (about 220° on a jelly thermometer). Spoon immediately into hot, dry, sterilized jars, being sure that the apples are fairly evenly divided among the jars. Discard the spice bag. Seal the jars and process in a water bath for 5 to 10 minutes.

I much prefer the mixed pickling spices for apple preserves. In fact, I think it is the sort of hot undertaste that this spice gives that makes apple preserves so intriguing. If you are not looking for adventure, then the whole cloves might be a good idea. Mammy Dossett used mixed pickling spices.

Apples were also dried. To prepare **dried apples** in the traditional manner is easy. Good tart apples—Wolf River, Granny Smith—are peeled, cored, and sliced thin. They are then spread in a single layer on a clean, white cloth on a table in the full sun for three or four days until they are dry. Turning them occasionally to be sure that all sides are exposed to the sun is a good idea but not essential. It is necessary, of course, to bring them in at night or to cover them with a cloth and then a sheet of plastic so they don't get wet with dew. After three or four days, the apples can be put into a clean, white bag for storage. To be absolutely sure the apples are dry, it is a good idea to allow them to stay overnight in an oven which has been warmed and turned off. In fact, you may want to do this each night for several days. If properly dried, the apple slices should rattle when the bag in which they are stored is shaken. By the way, if you are squeamish about flies getting on the drying apples, an easy cover can be made by fastening screen wire to an open box made of 1-inch lathing which has been joined together to make a frame the size of your table. You can also spread another white cloth over the apples, but that will slow the drying some.

There is really no substitute for home-dried apples. Commercially dried apples have been treated to make them stay white, but the preservative makes them taste altogether different from home-dried ones. I haven't tried the new drying boxes that are made for the oven, but I believe they would work if you don't use the chemical crystals which come with them. It is a simple fact that home-dried apples turn dark. Accept it and enjoy their wonderful taste. Without them, you can't make dried apple fried pies, you can't spread them on tea cakes, and you certainly can't make apple stack cake. They are worth the trouble.

We'll talk about apple stack cake and tea cakes later, but now is as good a time as any to talk about fried apple pies. I should warn you that making fried apple pies is an art which must be learned through careful practice. One wrong move and you have apples all over the kitchen. I wish I could make the recipe easier. Thus far I've found no easy way to do it for me, so how could I be expected to make it easy for you?

Fried Apple Pies

The crust:

2 cups all-purpose flour

⅓ cup shortening (remember, this used to be lard)

1 teaspoon salt

1 teaspoon baking powder

¾ cup milk

The filling:

2 cups dried apples

2 cups water

½ cup sugar

½ teaspoon cinnamon

Wash the apples in warm water. Drain off the water and place the apples in a heavy saucepan with water. Bring to a boil, then reduce the heat and simmer slowly until the apples have absorbed the water and are very tender. Stir in the sugar and cinnamon. Cool a spoonful and taste to see if additional sugar is needed. The apples should be very thick. If they are not, continue to simmer until they are very thick. Set aside to cool.

Place the flour in a mixing bowl and combine with the salt and baking powder. Cut the shortening in thoroughly. Mix in the milk to make a thick dough. Turn onto a heavily floured surface and knead in additional flour until the dough is stiff, smooth, and very firm. Divide the dough into 8 equal pieces. Roll each piece into a circle about 6 inches across, keeping the dough very thin on the edges but allowing it to remain thicker in the center. Place about ⅛ of the apples on the dough slightly off-center, spreading them to about 1 inch from the edge of that half of the circle. Fold over the other half of the circle and seal the edges completely by pinching the two pieces of dough into a neatly rolled edge.

Heat a flat griddle and coat with a tablespoon of butter or bacon grease (I strongly prefer butter). The griddle should be at medium heat and be maintained at as steady a temperature as possible. Place the pie on the griddle and allow it to cook about 10 minutes or until nicely browned. (While you are frying this pie, finish preparing the rest of them and start them cooking.) Turn and brown the other side. It is important that the pie not cook too quickly or the crust will brown before it has cooked through. Handle the pies very carefully to avoid breaking the pastry. Place on a warm plate and serve warm. You may find that folks will start eating before you have finished frying, but that is the chance you take. Be sure to hide one pie for your own pleasure. After so much trouble, you have earned it.

Another fine treat which was made in the fall was pear honey. This recipe uses the big hard "horse" pears common in East Tennessee and is not good made with Bartlett or other sweet, highly refined pears.

Pear Honey

6 cups ground pears
5 cups sugar
4 cups crushed pineapple

After peeling the pears and removing their cores, grind them through the coarse blade on a food chopper or a sausage mill. Mix the pears and the sugar together, bringing them to a slow boil. Cook, stirring occasionally, until they start to thicken. Add the pineapple, bring back to a boil, and continue to cook until thick and syrupy. Pour into hot, dry, sterilized jars. Seal and process.

Sorghum molasses is made in the fall—usually in September. I am told that on the day I was born, my father had worked all day at a neighbor's place, where they were grinding cane and making molasses. I can remember as a child hearing people ask if I was the child who was born at "'lassie"-making time. I was and I am. Back then, making molasses was a real event. Not everyone wanted or needed the equipment for making molasses. But almost all the neighbors grew a little sorghum cane so they could have their own molasses.

At our house, we planted a few rows of sorghum along the edge of the garden. In the fall, you cut your cane and hauled it on a scheduled day to the neighbor who had the mill and the cooker and spent the day while your cane was ground and the ugly green juice was boiled down as it flowed through a series of connected pans to make the rich brown syrup called molasses.

The cane mill was operated usually by mule power. It required a mule hooked to a long pole to walk in endless circles; the other end of the pole was attached to the mill and caused the upright wheels in the mill to turn. Someone sat near the mill, low enough not to get hit by the turning pole, and fed the cane into the mill. There it was crushed by the wheels, and the juice ran out the bottom into a pan. From here, it was poured into the top pan of the cooker and brought to a low boil. As it continued to cook and thicken, it was poured from one pan to the next at the critical point. In the meantime, the green foam which rose to the top was skimmed off by folks who tended the pans. It was important that the juice be kept hot enough but never get too hot, so someone with considerable skill was needed to tend the wood fire. Wood had to be kept ready, utensils had to be kept clean, and the mule had to be kept going in circles. It was a long, slow process which required a lot of folks to share the work, tell stories, eat and generally have a good time. I guess "'lassie"-making time was not such a bad time to come into the world.

Some folks cooked with molasses. Some used it to flavor

cakes and pies. Molasses could also be made into taffy. But mostly it was made to bring a welcome touch of sweetness to almost any meal. If you want to experience molasses in the finest and most traditional way, put a couple of spoonfuls onto a clean spot on your plate toward the end of a meal. Put about a tablespoonful of cold butter into the molasses, and with a fork completely work the butter into the molasses. You then place the mixture onto a piece of warm cornbread and enjoy. This is a ritual which my wife regularly enjoys while telling me she does it that way because it reminds her of her father rather than because she likes it that way. She doesn't fool me for a second.

Old-Fashioned Molasses Taffy

3 cups light brown sugar	2 tablespoons butter
1 cup molasses	¼ teaspoon baking soda
2 tablespoons vinegar	

Cook the first four ingredients slowly until a bit dropped into cold water forms a brittle thread (about 260° on a candy thermometer). Stir in the soda and beat to blend thoroughly. Pour into a large buttered flat pan (or, better, onto a buttered marble slab) and allow to cool until just cool enough to handle. It should still feel hot when touched. Butter your hands, pick up the candy, and stretch it. Fold it over and stretch it again. Continue to fold and pull until the taffy becomes a light cream color and starts to lose its stickiness. Stretch it into a long strip and cut into pieces with buttered scissors or a sharp knife. Store in an airtight box.

This recipe is a combination of one from my grandmother and one from her cousin, Ruth Montgomery. Ruth says it and a couple of other recipes I have used come from a cookbook which belonged to her mother.

The major event of the fall in East Tennessee and in most of rural America was the county (or state or regional) fair. In East Tennessee, the Tennessee Valley Agricultural and Industrial Fair has been going on as long as I can remember. Since my birthday is in September, my Grandmother Freeman took me to the fair as a birthday gift. She loved the fair and would have run away with the midway company if she had had the nerve. Actually, she had done just that when she was a young woman, and she still knew some of the people who worked the various midways. I was fascinated that my grandmother was a personal friend of Zola Williams, the world's only bearded fat lady (I personally met Mrs. Williams and can tell you that she was truly fat and was truly bearded).

Because of my grandmother, I also got to meet ticket sellers and balloon sellers. I even got to work a couple of years as a balloon seller myself. I met managers and midgets and the assorted other folks who make up a traveling midway company. With such interesting experiences, is it any wonder that I loved the fair?

But for serious-minded farmers and their wives, the midway was just a distraction. They went to the fair to show their finest stock or their best corn or their prize canned goods or their best rooster. If you went to the fair with my mother rather than my grandmother, you saw all those things and you exclaimed over them and wondered how they got the beans all in a line in the jar or how the corn always grew in exactly the same number of rows. You then went to one of the food stands operated by a church and ate white beans and cornbread (which, strangely enough, always tasted better there than the same thing did at home), or you might even get a dip dog from Nan Denton's stand, or popcorn or a candy apple. You got only one or two of those foods because money was always scarce. And then it was very late, and you would get on the bus or someone would pick you up at a gate and take you home. You were exhausted but certain you couldn't wait a full year for the next fair.

Besides the fair, a special treat in the fall was pumpkin. We had pumpkins of all varieties, including cushaws. (A cushaw, in case you don't know, is a large, strangely shaped green and white member of the pumpkin family. Their flesh is lighter colored and slightly sweeter than pumpkin but can be used in the same ways.) Because they grow on vines that can run for hundreds of feet, pumpkins had to be grown where there was plenty of room. This made cornfields perfect. It's not just artistic imagination that made shocks of cornstalks, surrounded by pumpkins, a symbol of autumn—they actually grew that way.

Pumpkins kept in a cool, dry place will keep for months if they are allowed to mature on the vine. This is a very good thing, because I know of no truly good way to preserve pumpkin. Today you can get commercially canned pumpkin, which isn't bad, or you can freeze it. But in my youth we never tried to can it ourselves, and we didn't have freezers then. We just kept pumpkins in the smokehouse or in the cellar and ate them before they rotted.

The traditional way of **preparing pumpkins** was a pain. In fact, because of the difficulty of peeling off the hard shell, cut fingers were almost an inevitable part of preparing pumpkin. If you are adventurous, you can still prepare it that way. Buy a medium sized pumpkin (or a larger one if you insist—after all, they're *your* fingers) and wash and dry it. Cut it vertically in two and with a large spoon scrape out all the seeds and the membrane which surrounds the seeds. Cut the pumpkin into long strips along the vertical axis with each strip about 1 to 1½ inches wide. Carefully cut the hard rind off each strip and cut the strips into roughly square pieces. Place in a large pan with a tight cover. Add a little water (about a cup of water for each 6 to 8 cups of cut pumpkin), cover, and bring to a boil. Reduce the heat and allow to cook slowly until tender, stirring occasionally. The pumpkin should be soft enough to mash completely.

There is an easier way. When you have split the pumpkin and removed the seeds and seed membrane, cut deeply through the flesh of the pumpkin as if you were cutting it into about 2-inch squares, but being careful not to cut through the hard skin. Place the pumpkin halves in a flat pan with the cut side up and cover the top of each half with a sheet of aluminum foil, pressing it tightly around the pumpkin. Bake it, covered this way, in a 300° oven for about 1 hour or until the pumpkin flesh comes easily off the shell. Scrape it out and discard the shell. The cutting into squares is important. If you omit this step, the cooked pumpkin will be in long, unpleasant strings and you will need to run it through a food processor or blender to break it up.

At this stage you are ready to proceed with any pumpkin recipe I know. You are also ready to freeze the pumpkin for later use. I simply measure the pumpkin into 1-cup batches and freeze it in plastic bags. It is then ready to thaw and use. The most familiar use of pumpkin was for pies. There are many variations on pumpkin pie, and you need simply to find the one you prefer. I have a favorite which is based on custom and on the fact that I like the taste of pumpkin. In too many cases, the flavor of the pumpkin disappears under layers of spice. But suit your own taste.

Traditional Pumpkin Pie

2 cups pumpkin   ½ cup milk or cream

2 eggs   ½ teaspoon ground nutmeg

½ cup sugar   pastry for a 1-crust pie (see p. 175)

¼ cup flour

Line an 8-inch pie pan with lard pastry. Mix together the eggs, pumpkin, sugar, milk, and nutmeg. Pour into the unbaked pie shell and bake on the lower rack in a 350° oven for about 30 minutes or until a knife inserted in the center of the pie comes out clean. This pie may be served hot or at room temperature.

Less Traditional Pumpkin Pie

2 cups pumpkin	½ teaspoon nutmeg
2 eggs	½ teaspoon allspice
¾ cup sugar	¼ teaspoon cloves
¾ cup milk or cream	pastry for a 1-crust pie (see p. 175)
½ cup flour	

Line a deep 9-inch pie pan with pastry. Mix together the eggs, pumpkin, sugar, milk, flour, and spices and pour into the unbaked pie shell. Bake about 45 minutes in a 350° oven on the lower rack until the center of the pie is firm and a knife inserted comes out clean.

My mother's family made a confection I haven't seen anywhere else, which they called **pumpkin custard**. A piece of pie crust was rolled thin and cut to fit an iron griddle. The griddle was heated with a little butter and the crust was fitted onto the hot griddle. A thin layer of pumpkin which had been sweetened and cooked down very thick was then spread onto the crust, and it was placed into a hot oven long enough to cook through. It was served while still hot. I was never sure why they didn't go on and make a pie, but they didn't. I do remember that pumpkin custard tasted pretty good.

In recent years, I have seen pumpkin made into **pumpkin butter**. It is made exactly like apple butter (see p. 93) except that it is flavored with whole nutmegs rather than cinnamon sticks. It is an interesting novelty and makes a nice gift with a loaf of pumpkin bread. I don't remember pumpkin bread when I was growing up, but my mother insists that she made it. I do know that the usual pumpkin bread is quick, easy, and very good toasted for breakfast.

Pumpkin Sweet Bread

1 cup pumpkin	2 cups flour
2 eggs	1 teaspoon baking soda
1 cup sugar	2 teaspoons baking powder
⅓ cup shortening	½ teaspoon salt
1 cup milk	1 teaspoon vanilla

Cream the shortening and sugar thoroughly. Add the eggs one at a time and continue to beat. Stir in the pumpkin. Sift the dry ingredients together. Add the milk and the dry ingredients alternately to the pumpkin mixture. Beat well. Stir in the vanilla. If you are feeling extravagant, add a cup of chopped pecans. Pour into a 9-by-5-by-3-inch loaf pan which has been greased and floured. Bake in a 350° oven for 45 minutes or until brown and firm to the touch.

For a pumpkin bread which is not a bit traditional but very good, try the following.

Not-a-Bit Traditional Pumpkin Bread

1 cup milk	½ teaspoon allspice
1 cup pumpkin	½ teaspoon ginger
¼ cup shortening	2 packages active dry yeast
¼ cup sugar	½ cup warm water
2 teaspoons salt	6½ cups all-purpose flour
1 teaspoon nutmeg	2 eggs

Scald the milk and stir in the pumpkin, shortening, sugar, salt, and spices. Cool to lukewarm. In a large mixing bowl or the large bowl of an electric mixer, sprinkle yeast on warm water and stir to dissolve. Add 3 cups flour, the milk mixture, and the eggs to the dissolved yeast. Beat until smooth. This will take about 2 minutes at medium speed with the electric mixer. Beat in the remaining flour a little at a time until you have a very stiff dough which leaves the sides of the bowl. Turn out onto a lightly floured surface and knead until smooth and elastic. When the dough has been kneaded enough, the surface will feel smooth and velvety and have a slightly blistered look. Place the dough in a greased bowl and turn the dough to coat it with grease. Cover and place in a warm place until doubled in bulk. Punch down and shape into two loaves and place into greased 9-by-5-by-3-inch loaf pans. Cover and allow to rise again until double in bulk. Place in a 375° oven and bake about 45 minutes until nicely browned. The top crust will be browner and smoother if you brush it with warm water about 10 minutes before it finishes baking. When the bread is done, it should sound hollow when tapped.

Just a passing word about hominy. Hominy is corn which has been allowed to mature fully and then is processed until it is tender again. Traditionally, the hard shell was removed by heating the corn carefully in a weak solution of lye. The corn was allowed to cool in the lye solution and then washed repeatedly with clear, cold water to remove all traces of the hulls and, of course, the lye. The resulting hominy was cooked, or dried to be cooked later. It was usually just boiled and buttered. Although the process of making hominy is of some interest for the history of foods, it is not worth trying at home. If you're not familiar with hominy, try the ordinary canned variety, which is perfectly acceptable. It's not bad with a good cheese sauce, but then sawdust wouldn't be too bad if you put a good enough cheese sauce on it.

You know, of course, that hominy is an altogether different thing from hominy grits. What they have in common is that they are made from corn, and this is the origin of the name. I should tell you that I never saw grits until I was grown. They were simply not a part of our diet. The closest we came to grits was cornmeal mush. Anyone can make mush. Not anyone can make it good.

Cornmeal Mush

1 cup plain cornmeal   3 cups water or milk   1 teaspoon salt

Bring the liquid to a boil and slowly beat the cornmeal into the boiling liquid. Continue to cook, stirring constantly until very thick (about 5 minutes).

At this stage you have a number of options. You can simply serve the mush in a bowl, like oatmeal, with butter, sugar, and milk (or any combination of these three you desire). On the other hand, you can make the mush at night and turn it into a greased loaf pan and allow it to stand covered in the refrigerator overnight. In the morning, turn it out and cut it into slices about ½ inch thick. Fry the slices in hot butter on a griddle until brown on the outside, turning the slices to brown them on both sides. You then serve the **hot fried mush** with syrup, molasses, jelly, or just sprinkled with sugar and cinnamon.

Better still, you could just go ahead and make one of the true delights of the Southeast,

Spoon Bread

1 cup plain cornmeal (yellow or white)	1 teaspoon salt
3 cups water	1 cup milk
2 eggs	bacon drippings or butter

Prepare cornmeal mush by bringing the water to a rolling boil, then beating the cornmeal into the boiling water a little at a time. Continue to cook, stirring constantly for about 5 minutes or until very thick. Allow to cool until just lukewarm. Beat in the eggs one at a time. Stir in the milk and salt. Pour into an ovenproof 2-quart casserole which has been coated with butter or bacon grease. Bake in a 350° oven about 45 minutes or until a knife inserted in the center comes out clean and the top is browned. Serve hot with plenty of butter.

These simple recipes represent as clearly as anything could that a cardinal rule of food in rural East Tennessee and in most other rural areas of our country in the 1930s and 1940s was to make the most out of what you have. M. F. K. Fisher wrote a wonderful cookbook about that time called *How To Cook A Wolf*. It was based on the premise that if a wolf is at the door, you have to learn to cook it. The East Tennessee folks I grew up knowing were experts at wolf cooking, and if you don't believe it, try fried mush some cold morning.

In the fall, our produce also included field peas. A number of these hardy species of peas were regularly grown in cornfields, much as green beans were, or became a regular part of the summer garden. The most common varieties were crowder peas, clay peas, and black-eyed peas. (I still see fresh field peas in markets sometimes, but they are becoming more and more unusual.) Field peas were eaten both fresh and dried. If they are picked young enough, crowder or clay peas can be broken like green beans and both the hulls and the peas cooked together. However, since the hulls become tough very quickly, these peas were more often shelled for cooking fresh.

If you are fortunate enough to see **field peas** on a farmer's market or in a supermarket, give them a try. Simply shell them and wash the peas. Place them in a heavy pot with a little water and a piece of fat pork, and cook them slowly until they are tender. Stir occasionally and add a little water if necessary. You can always find bags of dried black-eyed peas in grocery stores. We'll talk more about them when we get to winter food, but I should tell you now that I actually like them and eat them voluntarily.

As we finished with summer crops, we took off the old plants and cleared the ground for the green patch. In this area we sowed turnips, curly mustard, kale, and collards. Folks had their own preferences in greens, but almost everyone liked turnips, which they grew for both the greens and the roots. Various kinds of mustard greens were almost as common, and many people grew various varieties of kale. Not so many people grew collards, but they weren't unusual. Most folks cooked all kinds of greens together. You didn't have kale; you had "greens."

There are two basic schools of thought on how to cook **greens**. I can make a perfectly good case for either, so I give you both. The parboiling method, more common in my family, is not universally used. In fact, even in my family almost nothing is universally agreed on, and I think that is also a common characteristic of the folks in East Tennessee. On bad days I have been known to speculate on whether this area was settled by a roving band of anarchists and whether those traits might be transmitted genetically. At any rate, here are two authentic ways to cook greens.

The Boiling Method. Wash greens thoroughly through several changes of water. Pick over the greens carefully for any stray plant material or bad leaves which might have been inadvertently picked. Place the greens in a large kettle with water about ⅓ of the way up the side of the kettle. Place a piece of salt bacon on top of the greens. Cover and bring to a full boil. Reduce the heat but keep the pot boiling. Cook until tender and serve with the broth in which the greens cooked. This is called "pot likker." It is best eaten with hot cornbread. A little cider vinegar is traditionally poured over the greens in the bowl.

The Parboiling Method. Place well-washed greens in a large kettle with water. Bring to a hard boil and reduce the heat but keep the water boiling. Allow to cook about 30 minutes or until the greens just start to get tender. Drain. Fry several slices of salt bacon in an iron skillet large enough to hold the greens. Cook in the hot oil, stirring often until the greens are tender and all the water has cooked out. Serve hot with cider vinegar.

A couple of words might be in order about greens. First, there is no way to give you measurements for greens. Always put about six times as many greens as you want in the pot to start. They cook down a lot. Second, greens freeze beautifully (though of course this is not traditional lore). Cook them through the parboil stage, drain them, and place them in freezer containers. They will keep for months.

We can't consider greens without talking about **turnips**. They were traditionally peeled, sliced, boiled, and buttered. Sometimes a little sugar was added. Sometimes they were peeled, sliced or cubed, boiled lightly, and added to the greens when they had almost finished cooking. I have even seen them added to greens being cooked by the boiling method and allowed to cook directly with them. In short, there are lots of perfectly acceptable traditional ways of serving this tart and interesting vegetable. Turnips are also very good eaten raw, and I highly recommend them cut into small pieces and added to a green salad. If you have a favorite vegetable souffle, try substituting turnips which have been boiled, drained, and mashed for broccoli, spinach, or whatever you normally use.

If you've been paying attention, you've noticed that once again we're talking a lot about fruits and vegetables and not much about meat. This simply reflects the attitudes of the day. You lived on vegetables, and you ate meat when you had it. The notion that you need meat with every meal is a modern one in East Tennessee. Beef was especially uncommon. You didn't stop by the supermarket or the butcher shop on the way home to buy a steak, and if you did happen to pick up one, you didn't broil it and serve it rare. But in the fall, when the weather started to be cool, it was not unusual for someone to stop by and offer to sell you a part of a beef he had killed. This is how you took care of the storage problem. You killed a beef for your own use and sold off all you didn't have a place for. Instant stew and cash crop rolled into one!

In later years, the agricultural extension service made a great deal out of helping people learn to preserve more efficiently what they had produced. My family, being naturally progressive, was part of this. My father bought a pressure cooker fairly early, and my mother canned everything that she could get to stand still long enough. We had a special closet to hold canned goods. It was full when the summer was over. The cans came to include beef, cut into cubes (no matter what the cut was) and processed in the pressure cooker. Then it was available year-round for beef stew or simply to make beef and gravy.

The beef we got this way tended to be grass-fed and was often tough. This toughness combined with our conservative cooking habits to ensure that beef was fried, or boiled, or baked, or sometimes a combination of all three. It was always *well done*. I still find myself wanting country-style steak or Swiss steak or beef stew prepared as it was when I was a child. Rare prime rib it is not. Good it is.

Country-Fried Steak

3 to 4 pounds round steak

½ cup flour

1 tablespoon salt

1 tablespoon black pepper

 (or to taste)

2 tablespoons cooking oil

Trim all the fat off the steak, thoroughly pounding it with the back of a cleaver, the edge of a saucer, or a meat hammer and cut it into serving-size pieces. Mix the flour, salt, and pepper together and dredge the meat thoroughly with it. Heat the oil in a heavy skillet with a tight-fitting lid and when the oil is hot, brown each piece of the meat on both sides and then remove it from the pan. It will be necessary to brown it in batches. Keep the pan very hot but reduce the heat during the browning process if necessary to keep the flour in the pan from burning. When all the meat has been browned, return it all to the pan and add just enough water to cover the meat. Cover and reduce the heat enough to keep the water just boiling. Allow to cook about 1 hour or until the meat is tender. Remove the cover and if necessary allow to cook uncovered until the gravy which will have formed reaches the proper thickness. Serve hot.

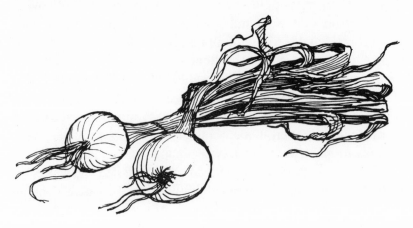

Swiss steak was a variation on this recipe. Some folks prepared it in much the same way and simply called it steak with tomato gravy. It's good, too.

Swiss Steak

3 to 4 pounds round steak	1 large onion
½ cup flour	1 cup cooked tomatoes
1 tablespoon salt	(canned ones are fine),
1 tablespoon pepper	coarsely chopped
(or to taste)	3 to 4 tablespoons cooking oil

Prepare the meat exactly as for country style steak. In the hot oil, first cook the onion until it begins to brown. Remove the onion from the oil and reserve. Brown the meat as for country-style steak. Return the onion to the pan; add the tomatoes and sufficient water to cover all the meat. Cover and cook until tender. Remove the cover and allow to cook down until as thick as desired.

Both of these dishes should be served with *real* mashed potatoes, hot biscuits, and green beans or turnip greens—and you should be prepared to overeat.

Beef was also boiled. You may have thought that this happened only in certain types of ethnic kitchens—folks from central Europe or the rural parts of France. Surprise! You can't imagine how disappointing it was for me to discover that "pot-au-feu" was just beef boiled the way my grandmother had done it. I wasn't crazy about it then, but my devotion to duty makes me report it to you. If you cook beef this way, you will find that the broth is delicious, and as for the meat, you will simply have to decide for yourself if you think it is wonderful or not. (In truth, a little boiled beef tucked into a biscuit isn't half bad. So much for sophistication.)

Boiled Beef

1 4- to 5-pound beef chuck roast   1 onion, 1 carrot, 1 stalk of celery

salt and pepper to taste   water

Sprinkle about 1 tablespoon salt into a heavy Dutch oven which has a tight fitting lid. Heat until hot enough for the grains of salt to start moving slightly. Add the meat all in one piece and brown on both sides. Sprinkle with the pepper. Add the whole onion and the carrot and celery which have been cut into large pieces. Add water to cover. Reduce to a bare simmer and cook until the meat is very tender. Place the meat on a hot platter to serve. Remove and discard the onion, carrot, and celery. If you wish, you may thicken the broth with 1 tablespoon flour for each cup of broth by mixing the flour thoroughly in a small amount of milk or water before stirring it into the hot broth. *Do not* try to mix the flour directly into the broth or you will understand lumps as you have never understood them before. If you prefer, the broth may be served plain.

It was also usual to add potatoes, carrots, and onions to the broth either during the cooking of the meat or after it was done, serving the vegetables with the meat. Turnips, cabbage, or parsnips were included sometimes. If you have decided that this sounds a lot like New England Boiled Dinner, you are right again. The only difference is that we served it with cornbread.

We also frequently made **beef stew**. To prepare it the way we did, simply follow the instructions for boiled beef above, except to cut the meat into 2-inch squares before you start to cook it. When the meat is almost tender, add your favorite vegetables, again cut into large pieces, and cook them with the meat. As with boiled beef, you may thicken the liquid or not, just as you please. The proportions given above will still work. Some debate continues over whether stew should have tomatoes. I prefer it without, but I have eaten very good stew with tomatoes. If you want to include them, put chopped canned tomatoes in with the original liquid so that they cook fully into the stew. I particularly like to include parsnips in stew. Their lovely, piquant flavor adds distinctiveness to the ordinary combination of potatoes, onions, carrots, and celery in most stews. But then the real association may be that I remember that Granny Weaver liked parsnips and put them in her stew.

In case you don't know, **parsnips** are vegetables that look like white carrots. They are fairly easy to find in produce departments, at least in the South, but commercial parsnips can't hold a candle to proper homegrown parsnips. Not only are parsnips one of those peculiar vegetables that have a long growing season, but even stranger, they become better if left in the ground to freeze before being served. If you have a flower bed with deep, loose soil, you may want to plant a few parsnip seeds in with your early radishes. The seeds sprout so slowly that the radishes will have come and gone by the time the parsnips arrive. Thin them to one about every 6 inches and leave them alone. The foliage is pleasant—something like a carrot top—and doesn't look bad mixed in with flowers. Do not cultivate. Do not fertilize. Leave them alone until the first real freeze of the winter has killed the tops. Then dig down carefully to find a succulent white parsnip. With good loose soil, the root could be as much as 3 inches across and 6 to 8 inches long. Traditionally, parsnips were peeled, cut into pieces, boiled, drained, and buttered. I find them a little strong flavored if cooked this way, but they are an excellent addition to stew or vegetable soup.

Now let's get back to meat. The basic fresh meat of the southern farm before freezers and supermarkets were common was chicken. As I mentioned earlier, this usually meant boiled chicken because once chickens get more than about six months old, they are too tough to fry. In the late spring and through most of the summer, you had fried chicken. The rest of the year you were condemned to chicken and dressing or chicken and dumplings. (This was not altogether a bad place to be condemned to.) Again, every cook had a special way of making dumplings that he or she felt sure was the best. The following is the way they were done in our family. I like this recipe.

Chicken and Dumplings

1 3- to 5-pound baking or stewing hen	1 small onion
1 carrot	salt
1 stalk of celery	water

Place the chicken in a large Dutch oven with a tight-fitting lid. Add the carrot and celery, which have been cut into large pieces, and the whole onion. Add water to cover. Bring to a full boil and skim off any gray foam which forms. Reduce the heat, cover, and allow to cook slowly until the meat begins to pull from the bones. Add salt to taste. Remove the chicken from the broth and allow to cool. Remove the meat from the bones and discard the skin and bones. Cut the meat into bite-sized pieces. Reserve. Remove the vegetables from the broth and discard. You should have about 8 cups of broth. Add water, if necessary, to arrive at this amount. Bring the broth back to a full boil, and add the dumplings (see below) slowly enough that the mixture never stops boiling. Reduce the heat, cover, and allow to cook slowly until the dumplings are done and the broth is thick. Stir the chicken back into the dumplings, adjust the seasoning, and serve hot.

Dumplings

3 cups plain flour	1 teaspoon salt
⅓ cup shortening	1 cup milk
2 teaspoons baking powder	

Mix the salt and baking powder with the flour; work the shortening thoroughly into the flour mixture. Add the milk and stir to form a firm dough. Turn out onto a heavily floured surface and knead until smooth (about 1 minute). Shape the dough into an even ball, flatten, and roll to about ⅛ inch thick. Cut crosswise into strips about 2 inches wide and cut each strip into pieces about 2 inches long. Drop into boiling broth as described above.

If the chicken is very fat, the broth sometimes has more fat than I care for. If so, I skim some or all of the fat off; I find that it adds little but calories to the dumplings. If you wish, the chicken can be cooked the day before and kept in the refrigerator until you are ready to do the dumplings. In that case, remove the chicken from the broth before you refrigerate it. You can then remove the hardened fat from the broth before you bring it back to a boil for the dumplings.

One of the common variations for dumplings was called "**slicks**." Simply prepare the dumplings as described above, but before cooking, spread the dumplings out on a clean dish towel and allow them to dry about an hour. Then proceed as above. This won't change the taste of the dumplings but will make a decided difference in their texture (as you can tell from their name).

Once again, every cook had a special way of preparing a dish like dumplings. One school of thought held that once all the dumplings were in the pot, the lid had to be put on and not removed for 30 minutes. Another specified cooking them without a lid and splashing them with cold water each of the three times the dumplings rose to the top. Theoretically, they didn't come to the top the fourth time, and this indicated that they were done. (I've since found out that the Chinese use the same method to ensure that their pork dumplings are cooked through.) Some East Tennessee cooks made dumplings very bland, and others added a good deal of black pepper. Again, there is no one correct way— it's a matter of taste.

Another favorite use for boiled chicken was chicken pie. My mother reminds me that at her grandmother's, chicken pie was as much a part of New Year's Day as black-eyed peas. Chicken pie is simple to make and delicious.

Chicken Pie

3 cups chicken broth

2 to 3 cups cooked chicken cut in bite-sized pieces

1 medium onion, peeled and chopped

2 carrots, peeled, sliced, and boiled lightly

1 cup green peas, cooked

4 tablespoons flour

salt and pepper to taste

crust for an 8-inch cobbler (see p. 175)

Thoroughly beat the flour into the cold chicken broth. Season with salt and pepper and bring to a boil over medium heat, stirring constantly. Add the chicken and the vegetables and bring back to a full boil. Taste and correct the seasoning if necessary. Place the bottom crust in a 2-to-3-inch-deep 8-inch-square pan. Add the filling and seal with a top crust. Pierce the top to allow the steam to escape. Bake in a 350° oven for about 45 minutes or until nicely browned. Serve hot.

I find it impossible to talk about chicken without also talking about dressing. Today, we think about dressing most in relation to turkey. When I was growing up, we sometimes had turkey, but chicken was far more usual. I still look on turkey largely as an excuse to have dressing. I've made an exception to this only since I discovered smoked turkey. We can't legitimately talk about it here because there is nothing traditional about it, but it is a delight. If you haven't had it, I recommend that you give it a try. You can find smoked turkey fairly often in the supermarket these days, and many barbecue restaurants smoke them during the holidays, but I personally would recommend that you buy one of the excellent home smokers now available. For the past several years, we have used a charcoal-burning model called the Cajun Cooker and have found it excellent. There are several other good brands around. Although gas and electric models are also available, someone who has both gas and charcoal smokers tells me the charcoal one is significantly better. I don't know. What I do know is that turkey, usually dry and bland, is moist and flavorful when cooked in one of those little jewels. But let's get back to traditional cooking and our discussion of chicken and dressing.

Dressing (and it was always "dressing," never "stuffing") was a way to use stale bread. You start with a combination of almost any kind of bread, mix it with seasonings and chicken or turkey broth, and bake it. The variations are infinite. But in the era when I was growing up, you could be sure that dressing would be a combination of biscuit and cornbread and would have sage in it. I should tell you that although I had been making dressing for thirty-five years, I had never measured anything until I started thinking about writing down a recipe. I simply crumbled up whatever bread I had and proceeded. I tasted the uncooked dressing to see if it was flavorful enough, and if it wasn't, I added more of whatever I felt it needed. If it is too flavorful, you have a problem, but, of course, that rarely happens. I say all that to remind you that the following recipe is a good place to start, but you shouldn't feel bound to stay there. Taste in dressing is so individual, in fact, that for family gatherings, my mother makes two pans full. One is always mild and the other hot. The following version is middle-of-the-road. You may vary it to suit your taste.

Dressing

4 cups cornbread crumbs

4 cups biscuit crumbs

2 medium onions, minced

4 stalks celery, cut into
small pieces

2 teaspoons black pepper

2 teaspoons salt

1 teaspoon ground cayenne pepper

1 to 2 tablespoons rubbed sage

2 cups water

4 cups hot chicken or turkey broth
(approximately)

Place the cut onion, celery, and water in a saucepan and bring to a boil. Place the crumbs and all other seasonings in a large mixing bowl and mix thoroughly. Add the boiling onion mixture and most of the hot broth. Mix thoroughly. The mixture should be soft but still hold its shape. Add more broth if necessary. Taste and add more seasonings if necessary. Remember, the cooked dressing will be slightly more seasoned than the uncooked mix. Place in a large, flat baking dish and bake in a 350° oven until browned and firm. May be served hot, cold, or warm.

Fall and winter were also the prime times for game. Rabbits, squirrel, and deer were the principal varieties which my family ate, but I have also heard of folks who liked 'possum. Rabbit was fried and steamed in much the same way as country fried steak. Squirrel was boiled and served with dumplings. Venison was cooked any way that beef was cooked. I didn't like any of it, and I don't see any reason to waste your time with it. If you're really interested in cooking game, there are a number of good books around for you to consult.

But since you may be curious, my cousin Ruth Montgomery has provided her mother's recipe for **'possum and sweet potatoes**. If you are interested, you must first get and clean "a nice fat 'possum." You then soak it overnight in salt water. You peel sweet potatoes, cut them into quarters, and put them in a covered roaster. Place the 'possum on top of the sweet potatoes, cover, and bake in a hot oven (about 375°) for two hours or until the 'possum is nicely browned. Salt well. To serve, arrange the sweet potatoes on a platter with the carved 'possum on top of them. The gravy which forms in the pan is poured over the meat and potatoes. According to this recipe, you won't need to thicken the gravy. (You won't find *me* cooking 'possum, though.)

I do like **dove**. In my family and my wife's, generally only the breast of the dove was eaten. In addition to frying it, it is necessary to steam it a little; it is very tasty but tends to be tough. I know of no commercial source of dove, but if you are fortunate enough to know a dove hunter, talk him out of about three or four breasts for each person to be served. Prepare them exactly as for fried chicken (see p. 80), covering the skillet to steam them while they are frying. Then make gravy in the grease. Excellent.

Sweet potatoes, a great treat, are an essential part of fall. A few years ago, when I lived for more than a year on Taiwan, nothing evoked the spirit of home more than smelling sweet potatoes cooking in a street vendor's jar. Many varieties were common when I was growing up, and I have found that you can still find several of them in the farmers' markets in this area. However, the big, sweet, yellow-fleshed variety which was always my favorite now seems to have largely taken over the market. Among the other kinds of sweet potatoes I remember was a red-skinned, white-fleshed variety. This long, thin potato was very flavorful but so dry that I was always sure I'd choke before I got one down.

Sweet potatoes were baked, boiled, and fried. They were eaten with butter, with gravy, and plain. They were sweetened, and they were made into pies. In any of these ways, they were good.

To fix a **baked sweet potato,** simply wash and dry it thoroughly and place it on a cookie sheet or directly onto the rack in a 350° oven and bake until it feels soft to the touch. This will take about 45 minutes to an hour for a medium-sized potato. Serve the potato hot with butter. I have found that as with Irish potatoes, using a potato nail gives the flesh of the sweet potato a softer, better texture. (However, I assure you that Mammy Dossett did not use potato nails.) Leftover baked sweet potatoes, unbuttered, are not bad cold. They can also be peeled, sliced, and reheated by baking with a little butter and sugar. Although this will look much like the classic candied sweet potato, the cooking method and the resulting texture of the potato are different.

Candied Sweet Potatoes

4 to 5 large sweet potatoes   ½ cup brown sugar
1 stick of butter

Peel the potatoes and cut them in large chunks. Boil in lightly salted water until just tender when stuck with a thin, sharp knife. Drain the potatoes and put into an ovenproof dish with a cover. Cut the butter into small pieces, distributing it evenly over the potatoes. Sprinkle evenly with the sugar. Cover and place in a 350° oven. After about 20 minutes, check to see that all the sugar has melted to form a syrup with the butter and any liquid from the potatoes. If it has not, turn the pieces of potato carefully so that no sugar is left on the top. Remove the cover and allow the syrup to cook down about another 10 minutes or until it is very thick. Stir the potatoes gently to coat with the syrup and serve immediately.

Another favorite at home was sweet potato pudding. It was a Sunday dish, and when things were going well, there were marshmallows to go on top of it. They aren't necessary but they don't hurt. Coconut is also nice as a topping, but that is a modern addition.

Sweet Potato Pudding

4 to 5 large sweet potatoes   2 eggs
½ cup butter or margarine   ½ cup milk or cream
½ cup sugar   1 teaspoon nutmeg

Peel the potatoes and cut them into eighths or smaller. Cook in lightly salted water until tender. Drain thoroughly and mash with a potato masher or with an electric mixer. When they are partially mashed, add all the other ingredients and mash and beat them thoroughly into the sweet potatoes. Turn into a buttered baking dish and smooth the top. Bake at 350° for about 25 minutes. Remove the pudding from the oven and brush the top with 4 tablespoons melted butter. Return to the oven for an additional 10 minutes or until browned and glazed. May be served hot, warm, or cold.

Variations. If you prefer a marshmallow topping, instead of brushing with butter, cover the top of the pudding with marshmallows and return it to the oven until the marshmallows have melted and are brown on top.

If you want to try the coconut topping, mix ½ cup flaked coconut with 4 tablespoons melted butter and sprinkle evenly over the potatoes and return to the oven until the coconut is brown.

No discussion of sweet potatoes would be complete without talking about sweet potato pie. As with pumpkin pie, every cook had a variation on sweet potato pie. One of the genuinely fine recipes I have found in the modern American cooking which is currently so popular is a **sweet potato–pecan pie** recipe developed by Paul Prudhomme. I thought about including that recipe, but clearing of the copyright is too much of a hassle, and I can't bring myself to follow the more common practice of changing one ingredient and including it without attribution. So if you haven't bought his cookbook, do so and see his modern adaptation of this traditional dessert. In case you don't have the price of the book and want to be adventuresome, put about half of the following filling into a partially baked pastry shell in a deep-dish pie pan and put a half recipe of a good pecan pie filling on the top before you bake it. It is delightful. Now back to the subject of traditional sweet potato pie.

Sweet Potato Pie

3 cups sweet potatoes, cooked and mashed	2 eggs
	½ cup milk
4 tablespoons butter, melted	½ teaspoon nutmeg
½ cup sugar	½ teaspoon allspice

Mix all the ingredients thoroughly and turn into an 8- or 9-inch unbaked pie shell (see p. 175). Smooth the top and bake at 350° about 45 minutes or until puffed and brown. This pie is good hot, warm, or cold. It is wonderful served warm with a dollop of ice cream or whipped cream.

When I was talking recently with Carol LeCompte about traditional foods, she asserted that I would surely include sweet potato biscuits in my discussion of sweet potatoes. (Carol now lives here in Knoxville, but she grew up in Louisiana and is a first rate Cajun cook.) She could hardly believe it when I told her that I'd never even heard of sweet potato biscuits and, therefore, couldn't possibly include them. But she straightaway enlightened me, and even if sweet potato biscuits aren't part of *my* tradition, they're so good I had to put them in.

Sweet Potato Biscuits

1 small sweet potato, baked (about ⅔ to 1 cup)	2 teaspoons baking powder
	¼ teaspoon salt
2 tablespoons butter	3 to 4 tablespoons milk
1 cup flour	

Peel and mash the sweet potato with the butter and cool. Mix the flour with the baking powder, salt, and milk to make a dough. Add to the potato and mix well. Turn onto a floured board and knead a few turns. Roll, cut, and bake on a greased cookie sheet in a 400° oven about 12 minutes or until brown. Should make about a dozen biscuits. Serve warm.

Since we have already wandered from the fold, let me give you one other sweet potato recipe which Carol gave me. This bread is terrific whether you use sweet potato or pumpkin. Since all the *ingredients* are part of my East Tennessee tradition, I think it's a legitimate addition.

Sweet Potato Cornbread

1½ cups whole wheat flour

5 teaspoons baking powder

¼ teaspoon cinnamon

¼ teaspoon allspice

½ teaspoon salt

1 cup cornmeal

½ cup soft butter

⅔ cup brown sugar

3 eggs

3 tablespoons lemon juice

1½ cups cooked, pureed sweet potatoes (or cooked, pureed pumpkin)

1 cup milk

Sift together the flour, baking powder, cinnamon, allspice, and salt. Stir in the cornmeal. Cream the soft butter until it is smooth. Beat in the sugar. Add the eggs and lemon juice and beat again until smooth. Thoroughly beat in the sweet potato (or pumpkin). Add the flour mixture alternately with the milk, continuing to beat well until everything is combined. Spoon the batter into 2 greased, 9-by-5-by-3-inch loaf pans and bake in a 350° oven for about an hour and a quarter or until a knife inserted in the center comes out clean. Allow to cool in the pan for about 5 minutes and then carefully turn the loaves out on a rack to cool. Good served warm or cold. Makes 2 loaves.

I have told you enough already for you to know that I come from careful, frugal folks who believe in not throwing anything away. One of the rituals of fall also proved that point. I have mentioned several times that no grease was ever thrown away. If bacon was fried, the grease was kept. If beef was boiled, the grease was taken off the broth and kept. If lard became rancid, it was still kept. All this stale, rancid grease became the basis of one of the essentials of farm living, the fabled lye soap.

By the time I came along, we went to Spradlin's store and bought Red Devil lye in a can. At the Weavers', though, the remains of a lye hopper could still be seen near the woodshed.

The traditional way of getting lye was to put wood ashes from the fireplace and the kitchen stove into a large container in the yard. Water was then poured into the container and allowed to run through the ashes. On its way through, it leached the natural lye out of the ashes. At the bottom, the water seeped through a narrow slot into a trough that led to a bucket. (This contraption was made entirely of wood because the lye would dissolve metal.)

For making soap, lye was mixed with more water and the rancid fat and heated in an iron kettle over an outside fire. The horrible brew in the kettle was then allowed to cool, and the soap rose to the top. After it had cooled thoroughly, the soap was cut up and these chunks air-dried for later use. I still remember sitting with Mammy Dossett in the cool of a fall evening while a small fire burned under the kettle which she stirred occasionally. I have no idea of the proportions or how she knew when it was soap. But she knew.

On this note, let's leave fall. It has been a busy time of hard work but good eating. East Tennessee is at its best in April and October. But now the leaves have fallen, the last of the crops are in, and the last canning jars are full. It may seem like we have nothing to do until spring, except survive, but let's not place any bets on it!

5
Winter

By now, you've no doubt gotten the idea that life on a subsistence farm in East Tennessee was hard and the work was constant. That they were. At the same time, I'm concerned that I may have overemphasized the difficulty. In fact, I sometimes think that the thirty years I have been away from the type of life that I'm talking about may have so softened the memory of it that I make it sound too sweet. I've already told you that I hated *The Waltons* on TV. All that sweetness and kindness and loving being barely able to get by elevated my blood sugar if I just turned past the show on the dial. I don't remember life that way at all. (My mother, however, still remembers the farm in terms so loving that it makes *The Waltons* sound bad.) So I try to balance the memories of how miserable it was to slop the hogs on a cold morning with how wonderful it was to feel the self-sufficiency of having food which you had raised, preserved, and prepared. You'll just have to weigh the evidence and judge for yourself how much of my account is real and how much is prejudice.

All this leads into winter. Now that you've been through three seasons of hard work and good food with me, you may think winter will turn out to be a time of respite, a time for us to rest and plan for spring planting while we eat the fruits of all our labor of the previous seasons. It wasn't that way at all—we couldn't just sit back and eat the apple butter we made the previous summer. Winter didn't mean that chores stopped for three months. Cows still had to be milked and chickens had to be fed. Gathering eggs and all the other daily tasks went on all year round. Maybe the men on a farm had it easier in the winter because plowing and planting and harvesting were over, but the women in the kitchen had constant work, no matter what the season.

There was work for the men in the winter, too, though of a different sort. What I remember most from the winters of my childhood was hog killing. My father helped people throughout the community with their hog killing and preparation in the years that he worked exclusively on the farm. It was a way to supplement his income. I can remember going with him and standing near the pig lot or pig pen and watching him shoot the pigs, stick them, and help with the butchering. Like molasses making, hog killing was a complicated process—something that a group of people working together could accomplish, though it would have been almost impossible if they had tried to do it individually.

Hog killing was part of our common folklore. I'm fond of a tale about hog killing that I got from a former Tennessee politician. He'd heard of a county school superintendent, about to be up for reelection, who was campaigning from farm to farm at hog killing time. At one of his stops, after he had a little too much to drink with his constituents, he lost his balance and fell into the fire under the vat where they were scalding hogs. One old country fellow simply stood there watching, clutching a broom while the others put out the man's clothes. Later one of the other men said, "You were standing closest when he caught fire; why didn't you try to use that broom to put him out?" The man thought a moment and said, "I thought about it, but it didn't seem right for an uneducated man like me to be beating on a college graduate with a broom."

I remember very fondly the time of the butchering of hogs and the preparation of the meat. Maybe this is because I was seldom involved in the really hard, dirty part of the work but always participated in the good eating that came along with the process. After a hog was either shot or otherwise knocked down, its jugular was cut and the carcass was hung so it could bleed thoroughly. Then it was scalded—sometimes in a vat made specifically for the purpose, sometimes in a makeshift contrivance. I can remember seeing a 55-gallon drum, partly sunk in the ground at an angle, being used. A hog weighing several hundred pounds had to be dipped first from one end and then pulled out, turned around, and dipped again. Isn't it wonderful that I remember watching this being done rather than remember doing it? I also remember that my mother's uncle, C. D. Weaver, had a large tank built over a fire pit into which the largest hog could be put, and there was only the job of getting the hog into the tank, rolling it over, and getting it out again. If the hog had been properly scalded, the hair could then be scraped right off. See how easy this all is? Think about it the next time you stop by the supermarket for some sliced bacon.

Because of the difficulty involved in this procedure and the need for special equipment, it was not uncommon for people to hire someone to do the work of killing and cleaning a hog up to the point of having a clean carcass or even through the stage of "blocking out" the hog into the large main pieces. From this stage, there was still a lot to be done. The pieces had to be trimmed to an established shape and the trimmings divided into fat and lean. Sausage was made from the lean "with enough fat added to fry it," and the fat was cut up to be rendered into lard. The backbone, ribs, and tenderloin were put aside to be eaten fresh. The head—perhaps the feet and tail—were to be made into souse meat and the liver into what was called "liver pudding" or "liver cheese." While hog killing meant a lot of work, it also meant having pork for the next year.

Even though I doubt that you will want to rush out and buy a whole carcass or even a hog's head and liver to prepare, I think that in this day of mass-produced country hams and water-injected bacon, it still would be good to remember the old traditions. On the farm, the main pieces of the hog—two shoulders, two hams and two middlins, and sometimes the jowl—were cured with either salt or sugar. Every farmer was sure he or she had the only real way to cure meat. The easiest way was simply to pack the meat in salt on a bench in an unheated area, letting it lie there for six weeks to "take the salt." For this process to work correctly, the weather had to be cold enough that the meat would not spoil but not so cold that it would freeze. Seldom, though, was this simplest method followed. Most folks seasoned the meat with some combination of salt, sugar, brown sugar, and black pepper or other spices to achieve just the taste they wanted. Their techniques varied. Some spread the meat on a bench with a thin layer of these curing agents all around the pieces of meat, and some packed them down into a box made for the purpose. Some people added sodium nitrate (saltpeter) to the mixture. Although today there is controversy about whether sodium nitrate is safe to eat, it is undisputed that it helps the meat retain its color.

Whatever curing agents and whatever application methods were used, the curing period was for about six weeks to two months. After the curing material was removed, the meat was washed and hung to age further. Sometimes it was hung in a cloth bag. Sometimes it was just hung from a rafter. Some people smoked the meat; most did not. Mammy Dossett's smokehouse was built with small hinged doors in the eaves of the building which could be closed to smoke meat in it. (I remember it being done only once.)

Anytime after the minimum six weeks of curing, this meat was ready to start to be eaten. Whether it was better immediately or after it had hung for a while was another of those topics everyone disagreed about. However, most folks did not have the luxury of having it hang around for a year to achieve that just-right taste and texture that some self-styled experts now demand. I can remember that the first hog killing was often at Thanksgiving and that one ham or shoulder was set aside in the curing process to wash and bake at Christmas. (Because I remember that half-cured ham as being delicious, I keep intending to try to recreate it.)

Once you had this primary task of getting the large pieces of the meat taken care of, all the rest had to be processed. In the traditional East Tennessee way of cutting pork, the backbone was not split to produce pork chops. Instead, the ribs were cut off at each side of the backbone with the bone and the meat near it cut in chunks. The wonderful lean strip of pork which makes up the center of a pork chop was stripped out in a single piece called the **tenderloin**. I remember it principally as a breakfast food. It was sliced crosswise into slices about a quarter of an inch thick and fried in a hot iron skillet. Milk gravy (see p. 82) was then made in the pan and served with hot biscuits (see pp. 162–65). This is still one of my favorite breakfasts for a lazy Saturday morning. A few times recently I have seen pieces of pork loin in fine butcher shops. But you can simply use good center-cut pork chops for the tenderloin. When I cook it, I cut as much fat as possible off before frying the pork and fry that fat out first to produce the grease in which I fry the lean meat. Frying needs to be done at a fairly high temperature to ensure that enough brown bits will stick to the skillet to provide a good gravy. If you want to try this, you may find that you will need to add a little oil in order to make the gravy —today's pork is very lean.

Most often the backbones and ribs were boiled and then cooked with vegetables or with homemade kraut. I still absolutely love backbones, ribs, and kraut. If you can't find backbones in the grocery store, you can make this dish just with ribs. If you get desperate to see what it was like, you can even do it with fresh pork shoulder, but that's cheating a little.

Ribs and Kraut

3 pounds meaty pork ribs, backbones, or any combination thereof

1 medium onion, peeled and left whole

1 quart homemade sauerkraut or two 16-ounce cans of commercial
   chopped kraut

Place the meat, cut into large pieces, in a heavy Dutch oven with about two cups of water. Add the onion and bring to a full boil. Skim off any foam which forms. Reduce the heat, cover, and boil lightly until the meat is fully cooked. Remove and discard the onion. Add the kraut (if you use commercial kraut, be sure to drain it) and allow it to continue to cook uncovered about 30 minutes or until the kraut has cooked through and the flavors have blended. The broth should have cooked down to a fairly small amount and be fairly thick. If not, allow it to cook down a little further. Serve hot with cornbread.

Butchering wasn't finished until we rendered the pork lard, the essential cooking fat used throughout the year. To prepare the lard, you cut the pure fat meat into cubes about an inch square and cooked it fairly slowly, usually in a large cast-iron pot over an open fire, to render out all the fat. Then you strained it into lard cans for storage until it was needed. When you rendered lard, it was important to know what you were doing. If you cooked it too fast, it could scorch and have a bad taste. It was imperative that no water get into it at any point in the process, or it would become rancid. It had to be cooked in a way that produced pure, white, tasteless fat.

The skins were also rendered for their fat, but that was done separately. The skin was removed with as little attached fat as possible, cut into pieces, placed in a flat pan in a slow oven, and cooked off. The fat was drained off as the skins released it. This process produced the crisp, lightly browned pork skins which became a snack in their own right. By removing the skins and cooking them by themselves, you also produced cracklings that were wonderful for cracklin' bread. I am sorry to tell you that all the commercial cracklings which I see in the stores these days have been rendered with the skin on, and to make them into cracklin' bread is a risky business. Sometimes skins render crisp; sometimes they just get hard. If you use cracklings which have had the skins left on, you must be prepared periodically to bite into something about the consistency of buckshot. Your alternatives are to go through and trim the skin off each piece or to make your own cracklings.

The latter part of the preceding paragraph was a quiz designed to see if you had any idea what a "cracklin'" is. While looking at one of the leading food magazines the other day, I saw a serious letter from a reader who said that in studying the new American cuisine, she had often seen recipes calling for the addition of cracklings. "What are cracklings?" she asked. To a proper East Tennessean, that's a shocking display of ignorance: Everyone should know that when you remove the fat from fat meat, what you have left is a cracklin' (you may decide for yourself if it is supposed to have a *g* on it). The new American cuisine has discovered that cracklings, cooked correctly and thoroughly drained of the fat, can be an interesting addition to salads or breads. We knew that in East Tennessee a long, long time before they discovered it. Now that I've made sure you know what cracklings are, all we need to do is settle on the fine points of what constitutes good ones. If you haven't had the pleasure of eating cracklin' cornbread, I recommend it to you. Simply pick your favorite cornbread recipe (see pp. 168–69), add about a cup of cracklings to it, and bake as directed. It is an excellent accompaniment for a meal of pinto beans and turnip greens.

The making of **cracklings** for this recipe is really an easy process. Simply buy a piece of uncured pork with a considerable amount of fat on it or ask your butcher for a piece of pure, fat, uncured pork (it usually gets trimmed off and thrown away; you might get it free). Cut it into about a ¾-inch dice and put it on the stove in a heavy pan over medium heat. Stir until enough fat has rendered to allow it to start to fry. Reduce the heat until you can barely see the fat in the skillet move and allow it to cook slowly until the pieces of fat have become very lightly browned. Don't cook it too fast. When the pieces of meat are brown, drain off the grease (you will have produced pure lard) and drain the cracklings thoroughly. I put them in a strainer and place it over a bowl. When they are thoroughly drained, you are ready for cracklin' bread which will regain your heritage beyond your wildest dreams.

I'm not going to trap you in an unending set of hog-killing trivia forever, but I do want to mention one more example of how we didn't waste anything from the hog. When the lard was being rendered outside over a wood fire, it had to be stirred almost constantly. One diversion was to cook the "melt" from the hog in the boiling lard and have it with bread as a snack while you cooked. If you aren't thrilled with the idea of eating any of the internal organs of any animal, you probably don't want to know that I have since learned that the "melt" was the pancreas. It was trimmed and dropped into the cooking lard, fished out when it had cooked through, sliced crosswise and eaten with bread. It tasted like very mild liver and had about the same texture.

Another major task was the sausage-making. We had a big old-fashioned sausage grinder which my father had mounted permanently on a board. In the fall it was brought out, cleaned up, and made ready for its annual task. When the meat had all been trimmed, the lean scraps were put aside with a little fat. I believe that at our house the proportion was probably about 90 percent lean to 10 percent fat. I know we had lean sausage. I am amused by the current "whole hog" sausage folks who love to tell you that the hams and shoulders are included in their sausage. They certainly are, but then so is the lard. It's funny how things like that work out. For sausage-making at our house, the board with the sausage grinder was placed between two chairs, and two people faced each other across the machine, one cranking and the other putting meat into it. It was a convivial way to get the job done. (In fairness, I must tell you that the device I just described was the only one of its sort I ever saw. When it wore out, we bought one that fastened on the edge of a table—but don't you like the other picture better?)

Once the meat was ground, it was mixed with salt, black pepper, red pepper, and sage. We had no real recipe for our sausage, and some of my fondest memories of the whole process are of our "experimental" method. After mixing fairly conservative amounts of the seasonings with the meat, we would fry a small piece of sausage to check the seasoning. A conference took place, and a decision was made on the correct amount of salt, pepper, sage, or whatever needed to be added. Then we fried another piece. The smell and the taste of that fresh sausage lingers still. There are lots of good commercial sausages on the market today, and sausage is still one of my favorite foods, but late at night when you had worked in the meat all day, the smell of sage and pepper and frying meat was far sweeter than any perfume, and the taste of the sausage, even when the seasoning was "not quite right," was wonderful.

I can't really recreate this experience for you—you had to be there. But you can experience the very special taste of fresh **sausage** if you want to. Simply buy a lean, uncured pork shoulder roast, and if you don't have a meat grinder, have it ground. For three pounds of meat, add about a teaspoon each of salt and black pepper, about 2 teaspoons of rubbed sage, and about ½ teaspoon of finely crushed dry red pepper. (If you must use commercially ground cayenne pepper, use a little less.) Fry a little piece of this sausage and see if it suits your taste. If not, just keep adding whatever you like best of the seasonings until you get what you like. I personally like the taste of sage far better than pepper, so I use less pepper and emphasize the sage. But, it's a matter of taste.

By the way, the sage we used (and which I use now) was home grown—it's far more flavorful than the commercial rubbed sage you buy. A couple of sage plants make a nice addition to a flower garden and will produce a considerable amount of sage. I particularly like the plain old blue-gray sage, but there are several bright-colored varieties—blue, green and white, and tricolor (red, white, and green)—which look attractive and have a good flavor for cooking. If you decide to try growing sage, it is an easy matter in the early fall to cut the sage branches, wash and dry them, tie them in bundles, and hang them upside down in a dark place to dry. Once they are dry, break off the leaves, discard the stems, and place the whole leaves in a jar with a tight-fitting lid. When you are ready to use the sage, simply rub some of the leaves between your fingertips to make the amount of sage you need. This way, it keeps its flavor much better.

But let's get back to sausage. A large hog will make a lot of sausage, and the life of fresh sausage with limited refrigeration is fairly short. Therefore, sausage was canned. (I report this only for the historical record and don't recommend that you try it. We did it out of necessity and not because it somehow tasted better: We simply had to can it or lose it.) First it was made into patties and fried. Then the fried pieces of sausage were packed into jars, and the grease which had fried out was distributed evenly among the jars. After the jars were sealed, they were turned upside down to allow the grease to pour to the top of the jar and seal the cans further as the grease cooled. The sausage kept very well this way, with a taste that didn't suffer too much in comparison with fresh.

We now arrive at the final chapter in the saga of the pig. Souse meat and liver sausage, or liver cheese—or liver pudding, as it was more commonly called in this area—used up what was left of the hog. Well, that's not exactly true. Some people cooked the pigs' feet separately and just ate them or else put them into jars with spices and vinegar to make pickled pigs' feet. Other people removed the brain before they made souse and had it scrambled with eggs. If you want to try **brains and eggs**, you start by cooking the brains lightly in fat in a skillet until the meat starts to break down into pieces (trust me—it *will* break down). Then you add beaten eggs and cook them until firm. People ate this for breakfast. If you're of such a mind, I'm sure you can find a butcher who will secure this delicacy for you. Take my word for it; it's not wonderful, but it's not nearly so bad as it sounds. After that digression, I return to my statement that souse meat and liver pudding took care of the rest of the hog.

Making **souse** began with cutting the head into large chunks, which were then put into a kettle with water to boil. (The jowl was often removed and cured.) The tail and feet were sometimes added to this pot. The meat was boiled slowly until it literally fell off the bones. This long, slow cooking process was important because it released the natural gelatin in the bones which was necessary for the souse to have a nice texture. Once the meat was cooked, it was allowed to cool in the broth. The next steps, however, gave rise to two divergent schools of thought about making souse. One method was for the cooks simply to pick through the mess with their hands, selecting all the lean meat and a little of the fat. This meat was broken into small chunks and put into a pot. A small amount of the broth was then added, along with salt, red pepper, and sage to taste, and the mixture was brought to a boil to mix the seasonings and to bring out their flavor. This mixture was then packed tightly in a loaf pan and allowed to cool. Some folks poured a layer of fat over the top to seal it. When cool, the gelatin got firm, and the souse could be cut into pretty slices with clear gelatin intermixed with pieces of meat. The second method called for picking out the meat, grinding it, and mixing it with a larger amount of broth, seasoning, and corn meal. Then it was cooked, with constant stirring, until it cleaned the sides of the pan. The final steps were the same as those of the other method: After being packed into a loaf pan (and sometimes sealed with a layer of fat), it was ready to be sliced and eaten cold or sliced and fried lightly. As with sausage, there is no way to give you a recipe if you want to try this difficult task. Souse needs about the same proportions of seasoning as sausage, but it's still a matter of taste. I cannot imagine that you will want to try making souse, but if you do, packing houses will often sell you hogs' heads cheap, and some will even give them to you. If you decide to try, do have the packing house or butcher cut the heads into quarters or smaller pieces for you. This is a difficult task that can't be done without a saw or an axe or some other heavy equipment that isn't part of the standard modern kitchen.

The liver isn't so hard to deal with, so you might want to try making a classic East Tennessee **liver pudding**. First you boil large pieces of pork liver until they are cooked through; this shouldn't take more than 15 or 20 minutes. Discard the water in which you cooked the liver. Grind the meat fine. Add about one cup of rich broth, which has *not* had the grease removed, for each two cups of liver. Traditionally the excess broth from the hog's head was used for this, and it was very rich and very greasy. The liver will absorb a lot of liquid (without it the pudding would be very dry). To the liver and broth add salt, red pepper, and sage; the proportions of seasonings we talked about for sausage will work fine for a start. Also add about ½ cup plain cornmeal for each 2 cups of liquid. Bring the mixture to a boil and cook, stirring constantly, until the mixture is thick enough to pull away from the sides of the pan. Pack firmly into a greased loaf pan and allow to cool. Serve cold.

We have now killed, cleaned, butchered, cooked, and cured a hog. You should be exhausted, and you have certainly earned the right to know still more about the good eating this strenuous activity produced. Best known of the products of this process is country ham. While the ham nowadays gets all the attention, there used to be little appreciable difference between the ham and the shoulder of the hog once it was cured. Today, other things are done with the shoulders and all most people think of is country ham. You should know by now that I am not a purist. I fully realize that I'm supposed to say that the only way to have good ham is to know some old mountaineer who cures his own and sells a few hams to get through the winter. If that myth makes you feel better, then you can persist in your belief, but I don't swallow it. I find that many commercially cured country hams are very good, and it is my general policy to acquire country hams by buying whatever is on sale at the supermarket. Of course, I'm lucky enough to live in East Tennessee. If you are so unfortunate as to live outside the Southeast, you may have to get your hams by mail order. There are many good, reliable companies around, and you can find them by checking the ads in some of the good, less pretentious food magazines. I, of course, prefer a ham cured in Tennessee to one cured anywhere else—chauvinism pure and simple that should be given no more weight than it deserves.

There may be a way to prepare country ham that isn't good, but I haven't found it yet and I've been looking at ways to prepare ham for a long time. The purest, simplest way to cook country ham is to slice and fry it. To **fry country ham** properly, you need a cast-iron skillet and it should be well seasoned. (By the way, if someone gives you a whole ham, forget tradition and ask your friendly butcher to slice it by machine. In the old days slicing was done by hand, and I could take a couple of pages and tell you how, but it isn't worth it.) When you are ready to fry the ham, soak the slices in hot water for a few minutes. Discard the water and dry the ham slices thoroughly. Trim as much fat as possible from the ham, put the fat in the cold skillet, and place it on high heat. Turning the pieces of fat as necessary, render all the fat out of it. Remove and discard the rendered meat. With the fat very hot, place as many slices as will fit flat on the bottom of the skillet into the hot fat and fry them until they brown; turn and brown on the other side and remove to a warm plate. Continue until all the ham has been fried. Do *not* layer it in the pan and be sure to keep the pan hot.

Once you have fried the ham, you are ready to prepare that masterpiece of southern culinary art, **red-eye gravy**. While making red-eye gravy is the essence of simplicity, there are several different formulas, each with its own ardent supporters. The truth of the matter is that how you make red-eye gravy depends on how much ham you are going to fry and how good the ham is. If you are frying a lot of good ham, all you need to do is get the skillet hot again after you have finished cooking the ham. Pour the fat from the skillet into a bowl; then add about a cup of water to the hot skillet, allowing it to cook all the accumulated brown bits off the skillet. When you pour the water into a properly heated skillet, it will steam and boil immediately. Continue to boil the liquid for a couple of minutes until it starts to look clear and thicken slightly. Pour it into the bowl with the grease, and you have made red-eye gravy.

If you have fried less ham or its quality has not been all you might have hoped for, there are a couple of tricks which will make your gravy look better and even enhance the taste a little. In fact, I have been known to use these two tricks together to produce a reasonably good red-eye gravy from just a couple of slices of ordinary ham. After the grease has been poured out of the hot skillet, you can sprinkle a couple of tablespoons of sugar into the skillet and allow it to caramelize before you add the liquid. This addition will improve both color and taste, especially if you are using salt-cured meat, which tends to be very salty. Some people also make red-eye gravy with coffee rather than water. It changes the taste slightly and improves the color greatly. You'll just have to try both ways to see which one you prefer. I haven't tried to give specific proportions, because I don't know any way to do it. You'll have to experiment. But please note that you will normally need very little liquid: To require as much as a cup of liquid for red-eye gravy, you will have to have fried a lot of ham in a big skillet.

Country ham is also wonderful baked. A number of companies will now ship country ham already fully cooked and ready to slice and serve. I have found that the two or three of these I have tried are very good but very expensive. Because it is so easy to cook a ham yourself, I see no reason for you to pay someone to do it for you. Traditionally, ham was heated in a large quantity of water and kept at a low temperature for a long period of time. This reduces the natural saltiness of country ham and restores moisture lost during the curing process. (For modern country ham, which is less salty and more moist, the recipe should be adjusted slightly.)

Perhaps the best known method of **cooking a country ham** is the "lard can" method. First the ham shank is removed and the ham is soaked and cleaned thoroughly; any excess fat is trimmed off. The ham is then put in a lard can and covered with water, which is brought to a boil. Next, the heat is turned off and the water is allowed to cool to lukewarm. If the ham is very old and salty, this water is discarded, but that will almost never be the case these days. The heat is then turned back on, the water is brought to a boil, and the heat is turned off. The ham is once more allowed to cool to lukewarm. It is then brought again to a boil. At this point, the can is removed from the heat and wrapped in several layers of blankets, newspapers, or some other material to insulate it. It is allowed to stand overnight. The next day the ham is removed from the liquid; once it has chilled thoroughly, it is ready to serve. The ham will keep for a couple of weeks in the refrigerator.

A much simpler process is to prepare the ham as described above, cover it with warm water, and allow it to soak overnight. Place it in a roaster pan with a tight-fitting cover. Cover the meat with water and bring it to a full boil. Then reduce the heat to the lowest possible setting which will keep the water barely simmering. Cook the ham about 10 minutes per pound and then allow it to cool in the broth. If you want the ham to have a nice, showy glaze, place the ham on a rack in a broiler pan and pack the outside of the ham with brown sugar which has been softened with pineapple juice. Bake in a 350° oven until the sugar melts and browns. You can garnish the ham with pineapple if it makes you feel better.

Now let me tell you about the method which I actually use for boiled country ham. Cut the piece of ham which you want to boil, and clean and soak it as described above. I have found that a small ham (12 to 15 pounds), properly trimmed and with the shank removed, works fine. Use a large Reynolds oven cooking bag, into which you place 2 tablespoons flour and about 1 cup of red wine. Close the bag with the twist tie provided and pierce 4 or 5 holes in the bag with a sharp knife. Place in a flat, uncovered roasting pan. Tuck in the end of the bag so it will not touch the walls of the oven. Bake the ham at 325° for about 15 minutes per pound. Then remove it from the oven and allow it to cool in the bag. After the ham has cooled, take it out of the bag and chill it thoroughly before attempting to slice it. Serve it, sliced thin, with hot biscuits.

If you use the oven cooking bag method, the drippings that remain in the bag are wonderfully thick and rich with ham flavor. They are great for seasoning either green or pinto beans. They can also be diluted about a third with water, heated to boiling, and served as a passable substitute for red-eye gravy. (You will know you cheated a little on it, and if any real old-timers come along, you may get caught, but it's sometimes worth the risk.)

I'm sure you've noticed by now that each time I've given you instructions on preparing a ham or shoulder, I've had you remove the ham shank. (Saw it off—or have your butcher do it.) If left on the ham, it just gets in the way. Removed, it becomes the basis for seasoning all sorts of things. It is wonderful cooked with dried beans. If cooked with a small amount of water, the ham shank and broth can be used to season canned green beans, or cooked with cabbage. It can also be used to make a dish that I haven't seen done outside my family. We reserve it as a special treat—one that seems to signal the last of the Christmas-to-New Year's holiday. We almost always have country ham as part of Christmas, and that means we have one or more ham shanks to make the rich broth for

Cornmeal Dumplings

4 cups plain cornmeal	2 cups hot ham broth (approximately)
1 teaspoon soda	ground cayenne pepper or chili powder
1 teaspoon baking powder	8 cups rich ham broth
½ teaspoon salt	(preferably from a country ham)

Place one or more country or commercial ham shanks (about 1½ or 2 pounds) in a large, heavy Dutch oven with about 12 cups of water. Bring to a boil, reduce the heat, and simmer until the meat starts to fall from the bones. Remove the meat from the broth; pick out all the lean meat and cut it into bite-sized pieces. Discard the bones and the fat and reserve the lean meat. Keep the broth hot but not boiling.

Place the cornmeal, soda, baking powder, and salt in a large mixing bowl and mix thoroughly. Stir 2 cups of hot broth all at once into the cornmeal mixture to make a dough that is just soft enough to hold together but still firm enough to retain its shape (add extra broth if necessary). Scoop up a piece of the damp meal mixture about the size of a small egg—this will be a generous tablespoonful. Shape this into a flat circle in your hand, and in the center of it place a generous sprinkle of the cayenne or chili powder. My mother still uses cayenne, and I love it. It is very hot. I find most people prefer to substitute about ⅛ teaspoon of chili powder for the cayenne. Fold the dumpling mixture over and completely seal the pepper inside it.

As you finish each dumpling, place it in a single layer on a plate lined with waxed paper. When you have finished making the dumplings, bring the remaining broth to a full boil and drop the dumplings into the boiling broth slowly enough that it does not stop boiling. With a large spoon, gently loosen any dumplings which may have stuck to the bottom of the pan. When all the dumplings have been placed in the broth, reduce the heat enough to maintain a slow boil. Cover and allow to cook for about 30 minutes or until the dumplings have cooked through and the broth is very thick. Stir the reserved ham back into the dumplings and serve hot.

I know this dish is heavy and fattening, but it's wonderful on a cold winter night. The mixture is also fairly versatile. I have been known simply to stir the pepper into the cornmeal mixture and then shape the dumplings when I didn't want to do it right. (I have also substituted rubbed sage for the pepper. It was all right for a change but not as good as I had hoped it would be.) I have also found that almost any good, rich broth will work fine. I recently made some very good dumplings with broth made from a smoked turkey carcass, some commercial ham, and a little country ham all mixed. The touch of smoke flavor was nice. Experiment a little.

As I mentioned a little earlier, ham shanks were also used to season dried beans. No account of food habits in East Tennessee would be complete without a discussion of the role of dried beans. If there was a single staple when I was growing up, it was dried beans. They might be white, pinto, or mixed, but they were always there. Every two or three days beans would be cooked, usually seasoned with fat salt pork; they were much better if cooked with a country ham (or shoulder) shank. Then they were reheated each day until they were gone and a new batch was started. I grew up believing that variety in the diet meant beans and potatoes one day and potatoes and beans the next. It may be hard for someone who grew up in a different culture (like my wife growing up in the heart of Park City) to realize, but it was expected that beans would be on the table every day, dinner and supper, no matter what else you had to eat. Given this heritage, is it any wonder that I still must occasionally find a pinto (or Great Northern) bean fix to make it through a hard week?

Even though East Tennessee humor tends to be a little strange (and often a little sexist), I ought to give you at least one bean story. It seems that a farmer came home after a hard day's work to see that supper consisted of pinto beans and corn-bread. He turned to his wife and asked, "Why are we having beans again tonight?" She thought for a moment and said, "I just don't understand you. You liked beans on Monday, Tuesday, Wednesday, Thursday, and Friday. Now suddenly on Saturday you don't like them anymore. I just don't understand you."

The cooking of **dried beans** is a simple, straightforward process. I personally prefer a mixture of pinto and white beans, but straight white beans or straight pintos aren't bad. To prepare this essential of life, wash a pound of dried beans, put them in a pot with enough water to cover them, and bring them to a boil. Immediately remove the pot from the heat and allow the beans to cool in the water. When the water is cool, drain the beans and again cover them with fresh water. Pick through the beans, removing and discarding any that appear discolored. (Also look for rocks.) Place the washed, picked-over beans into a heavy pan with a lid. Again cover with water and add a piece of salt-cured bacon about 3 inches long and 1 inch thick which has been cut almost through in a number of places. Bring to a boil, cover, and reduce the heat so that the beans just simmer. Cook about 2 hours or until the beans are soft and the broth starts to thicken. If the water becomes too low in the beans and they are still hard, add a little water and continue to cook. Just before serving, add salt to taste. (If your pork wasn't very salty, you may need to use a couple of teaspoonfuls.) Serve hot. If possible, cook the beans a day ahead, allow to cool, and refrigerate overnight. When you are ready to serve them, heat to a full boil and serve. I like the flavor of beans much better after they have stood overnight and been reheated. By the fourth or fifth reheating, they become a little strong but are still passable.

Dried beans cannot be truly enjoyed unless they are served with hot cornbread. If you like, the beans may be flavored with **pepper vinegar**. Fill a small bottle with your favorite kind of fresh, green hot pepper and pour boiling vinegar over it. Allow it to stand in the refrigerator for a couple of weeks and use the vinegar for flavor. When the first batch is used up, boil some more vinegar and start over. Use chow-chow, cucumber relish, or chopped raw onion with the beans. I prefer them straight with the cornbread crumbled into the beans. It may not be elegant, but it's good.

As I've mentioned, potatoes, like dried beans, were an ever-present staple. They were boiled, baked, and fried. They were eaten hot and cold. We used them so much because they were reasonably easy to grow and reasonably easy to save. There may be some people who don't like potatoes, but I haven't met them. I can't really claim that one means of cooking potatoes predominated over all the others. I also can't really say that they belong uniquely to winter—I've put them here because there is not a lot else going on, and they were available fresh when nothing else was. The new potatoes I mentioned in "Spring" are a delight, but properly done creamed potatoes or good home fries are always special.

My wife is convinced that mashed potatoes are an absolute cure-all. I know she is sick if she starts talking potato soup and that she is really sick if she suggests that all she could eat is mashed potatoes. We both have decided that the true test of any restaurant which claims to have country cooking is whether the potatoes are "real" or dried. (You may notice that I have talked about both "creamed" potatoes and "mashed" potatoes; I use the terms interchangeably. I don't talk about "whipped" potatoes.)

I think that probably the simplest and most common way (also the dullest) to have potatoes was peeled, boiled, and buttered. The next step was what I suppose should be called creamed potatoes. After the potatoes were boiled and buttered, fresh cream, salt, and pepper were stirred in, and they were heated and served.

The next step was

Mashed (Creamed) Potatoes

6 to 8 medium potatoes	¼ cup cream or milk (approximately)
water to cook	salt and pepper to taste
4 tablespoons butter	

Peel the potatoes and cut into small pieces. Cover with cold water and place on high heat. Bring to a boil, reduce the heat, and cook until the potatoes are tender. Drain, add butter and about half of the cream, and mash with a potato masher. (If you must, you can use the flat blade on a good mixer for mashing.) While mashing the potatoes, continue to add the cream until they reach a good consistency—still firm enough to hold their shape. Add salt and pepper to taste and serve hot.

When you make mashed potatoes, be sure to increase the recipe enough so that you have leftovers. If you don't, you can't make

Potato Cakes

2 to 3 cups cold leftover	½ cup flour, divided
mashed potatoes	butter or bacon grease
1 egg	for frying

Thoroughly mix the potatoes, egg, and about half the flour. Shape into small patties about 2 inches across and about ½ inch thick. Coat both sides with the additional flour. Preheat butter or grease on a griddle to medium heat. Fry the potato cakes until brown; turn and brown the other side. (It is important that your pan not be too hot or the cakes will brown on the outside before they have cooked through.) Serve hot.

Sometimes potato cakes were made without the egg. They were also sometimes made with egg and more milk to form a heavy batter which was poured like pancakes onto the hot griddle. The basic ingredient is cold leftover potatoes, and beyond that you should feel free to explore.

Potato soup was another of our universal dishes. I like a very simple straightforward soup but, as is often the case, there is considerable room for experimentation.

Potato Soup

6 to 8 potatoes	1 cup heavy cream
1 small onion	4 tablespoons butter
4 cups water	salt and pepper to taste

Peel the potatoes and cut them into very small pieces. Peel the onion and chop it fine. Put the potatoes, onion, and water into a heavy saucepan and cook until the potatoes start to cook up (that is, start to fall apart). Add the butter and cream and bring just back to a boil. Add salt and pepper and serve hot.

Variations. If you have the urge to jazz this up a little, use leeks instead of the onion and add a dollop of sour cream when you start to serve it.

Or, if you just can't leave well enough alone, increase the water about a cup and when the potatoes are cooking up nicely, add about 2 cups of cauliflower, and allow to cook just until the cauliflower is tender-crisp. Now add the butter and the cream, salt and pepper, and serve a first-rate **cream of cauliflower soup**.

If you just must, substitute commercial sour cream for the cream in the basic recipe and barely heat the potato soup. Do *not* allow it to boil.

See what happens when you even talk about potato soup? I'm sorry about these digressions. Sometimes, though, I just can't help myself.

Home-Fried Potatoes

6 to 8 potatoes   salt

1 large onion   bacon grease to fry

Peel the potatoes and slice thin. Soak the potatoes in cold water. Peel and slice the onion. Drain the potatoes and dry them. Heat 3 to 4 tablespoons bacon grease in a heavy (preferably cast-iron) skillet. Add the potatoes and the onion. Continue to cook at fairly high heat, turning the potatoes frequently as they brown. Cover between stirring. When the potatoes are tender, salt to taste and serve hot.

Everyone has a deep, dark secret that they would be embarrassed for their friends to know. Mine is that I like home-fried potatoes with mayonnaise. Please don't tell on me!

Even if potato salad is theoretically a summer dish, let's put it in here with the rest of the potatoes. It was a regular Sunday treat when I was growing up and I still love it. It was sometimes made with potatoes which were cut up and cooked and sometimes made with potatoes which were boiled in the jacket. This doesn't change the taste much, but it does change the texture of the potatoes. Try it both ways to see which you like better.

Potato Salad

about 8 cups of boiled potatoes

2 stalks celery, chopped fine

1 medium onion, chopped fine

4 hard-boiled eggs, cut into large pieces

¼ cup chopped sweet pickles
  (or sweet pickle relish)

¼ cup chopped dill pickles

4 tablespoons dill pickle
  vinegar

½ cup mayonnaise

¼ cup salad mustard

salt to taste

If you are using potatoes boiled in the jacket, peel them and dice them. If you peel the potatoes before cooking them, cut them into small pieces, cover with water, and boil until tender. Drain and continue with the recipe above. Add all the other ingredients and stir together. (You may want to adjust the amounts of mustard, vinegar, and salt to suit your taste.) Serve at room temperature. If any happens to be left, be sure to refrigerate it. Mayonnaise keeps poorly, especially when mixed with other things.

In the pre-mayonnaise days, wonderful potato salad was made with **clotted cream**. Add about ¼ cup of sugar and ¼ cup vinegar to 1 cup of heavy cream and substitute this for the mayonnaise and mustard in the recipe above.

One of my fondest memories from my youth was a dish we had about once a week throughout the year. Somehow, I associate it most with winter. I love rich, thick **vegetable soup**. I can't imagine getting through the winter without it. Although I can't give you a real recipe for vegetable soup, I will give you the principles, and you can try it for yourself. Some things are essential to good soup. First, it must have something to season it. A soup bone—ham or beef—or a chicken carcass will work. This must be cooked in water to make a stock. (You may remove the fat if you like.) Then you need a combination of vegetables which must include onion and tomatoes. It may also include okra, peas, corn, celery, cabbage, green pepper, carrots, parsnips or any combination thereof. It must have potatoes, spaghetti, macaroni, or some other kind of starch. These may be cooked new, but more likely they will be left over from earlier in the week. All of these ingredients are mixed together, salt and pepper added, and the soup is cooked most of the afternoon. The tomatoes for this kind of soup are the ones we talked about canning in "Spring." Remember, we also talked about soup mix then—corn, okra, and tomatoes. I wouldn't tell just anyone this, but commercially canned tomatoes and corn and commercially frozen okra (unbreaded) work just fine in soup. The secret of the best vegetable soup is a fine stock—along with putting in enough vegetables that you could be half finished eating before you notice it is soup. By the way, this kind of vegetable soup is good with saltine crackers, cornbread, or leftover biscuits which have been split and toasted.

Today we seem to make Christmas the big event of the winter, if not of the whole year. I don't remember it that way when I was growing up. It was important, but you didn't mortgage the farm for it. I really feel old when I say this, but I remember oranges at Christmas as a big deal. On Christmas Eve we went to Fairview Baptist Church, where every child (including me, even though my family weren't members of the church) received a nice little brown paper bag containing an orange and some hard candy. I liked that. I also remember going to look for a Christmas tree with my father and learning the fine points of selecting one that was not too large or too small, one that had a single top and a nice shape. It was, of course, a red cedar tree. It was brought in on Christmas Eve and was out before New Year's. (You may not know it, but it is very bad luck still to have Christmas decorations up on New Year's Day. We didn't mess with bad luck then and I still don't care to now.)

From time to time I've told you about the large number of people who ate at my Grandmother Dossett's on any Sunday. This number was multiplied on Christmas. All the aunts and uncles and great-aunts and great-uncles and cousins and their friends came on Christmas. Those half-cured hams I told you about earlier we ate at Christmas. We might also have chicken and dressing, chicken and dumplings, or both. (We might have boiled beef, too.) We always had biscuits and some kind of gravy and maybe cornbread as well. We certainly had mashed potatoes and canned green beans and maybe canned corn. Then we got down to the serious part of the meal, which would include three or four kinds of cake and two or three kinds of pie. Food was the central part of the celebration. While gifts tended to be small, simple, and personal, the meal tended to go on all day.

All of my life until I was no longer living with my parents (and even then if I was at their house at Christmas), it was understood that we would go to Mammy Dossett's for dinner. Everyone else had the same understanding. We still get together, but because there are so many of us (remember, I'm the oldest of eight children) and we all have children, we don't try for Christmas Day. But on the Sunday after Christmas, we each pack up enough food for everyone we know and go to one of our houses and spend the afternoon visiting and eating. You can always depend on several new dishes as well as many old favorites. Although we reached the point years ago that we no longer give gifts, we will not give up the pleasure of this meal together.

For the sake of an accurate historical picture, I need to mention one formerly important aspect of any big meal at a country home in East Tennessee. I'm not proposing a return to this custom, but accuracy requires that I at least report it. At picnics you would fill your plate from a big table and go sit on the ground somewhere to eat. That is as close to a buffet as we came. At real meals, the food was put on the table and you sat down to eat. Obviously, everyone couldn't get to the table at the same time. From this grew an order of precedence for eating. The men ate at the first table. There were no questions; there were no exceptions. Then the children ate, and then the women. If everyone could get at the table in two seatings, some of the male children would eat with the men, and the women and the rest of the children would eat together. The first time my city-raised wife went with me to a family gathering where this obviously "correct" practice was followed, she was incensed. Somehow, the fact that I had trouble knowing what she was upset about did nothing to improve the situation.

One last word before we leave the old year. New Year's Day meant **black-eyed peas cooked with hog jowl**. If you didn't have this dish, there was an excellent chance that your crops would fail and that you would be hungry before the year was out. I strongly advise staying with this custom. Bags of dried black-eyed peas are easy to find at the supermarket, and you cook them exactly the same way you cook pinto beans (see p. 146). I like to add a chopped onion and a pod of dry red pepper to black-eyed peas while they are cooking. It is necessary that peas for New Year's be coooked with cured hog jowl (this is one season you can easily find it at grocery stores). If you can find salt-cured rather than commercially cured meat, it is significantly better.

It wouldn't be right to talk about winter without mentioning the quilting and other kinds of sewing that were pursued in the long winter evenings. Mammy Dossett had a quilting frame which hung on cords from rings set into the dining room ceiling, so it could be raised up out of the way. Granny Weaver had hers on sawhorses which could be set up in the parlor. Both frames were designed so that a quilt could be put in the frame and left there until it was finished. As a result, the light in Mammy Dossett's dining room was dim when she had a quilt pulled up in the frame. I especially remember this as a part of winter.

The quilts themselves could take a number of forms. Many were traditional, with small pieces sewed together to make patterns like the various stars and log cabins and all the rest of the taxonomy of quilts. They might even be appliqued quilts like the Dutch Doll or the Kitten-in-the-Basket. We recently had a Kitten-in-the-Basket quilt finished by the quilting group at Fountain City Methodist Church, which my mother is a part of. She had embroidered the faces and made the squares, starting just after I was born. Mammy Dossett had set the squares together at least thirty years ago and the quilt top was put away unquilted. We now use it as a bedspread so everyone can enjoy seeing it.

The quilts might also be less elaborate—just squares or rectangles of cloth fitted together to make a bed cover. In fact, they were sometimes not quilted at all but simply "tacked" together with bright colored bits of thread at regular intervals. One of my real prizes in life is the last quilt which Mammy Dossett made for me, long after her eyesight was too bad to quilt. It is simply small squares of fabric on one side and larger rectangles on the other. She sewed the pieces together on the sewing machine. She then put in cotton filling and tacked it together with red and yellow threads which are knotted on the top sides.

In her later years, Ma Freeman devoted most of her spare time to the making of quilts and quilted toys which she sometimes sold but more often gave away. For all her grandchildren and great-grandchildren, they have become special remembrances of her. For my wife and me, she did a king-size quilt which is the "company" bedspread for our bed. But in the old days they were not made for keepsakes: a country quilt was made to use up scraps of material in a way that proved very practical in unheated bedrooms on cold winter nights.

And so we find our way through winter. In January you started thinking about planting. Tomato seeds could be planted in containers and put into the kitchen window by late February. Peas could be put out by the first of March. And the cycle begins again. Its beginning and ending are arbitrary. But we have to eat, and you might as well enjoy it. That's what the next chapter is about—good stuff!

6

Good Stuff

Whenever You Can Get It

No matter how much you try to impose order on things, somehow chaos always works its way to the edges, if not into the center, of them. Through the years as I thought about how I would like to organize my feelings and my recipes, I always knew that if you just worked your way through a year, you would obviously have covered everything and would be finished. This seems to have a wonderful, sort of simple-minded logic about it. And then I actually started writing this book. Within pages of the beginning, problems started to develop. Just when do you introduce the wonders of fresh hot bread? Cornbread isn't a feature of one particular season. Neither is blackberry jam cake. Then I was struck by a stroke of absolute genius.

Some things are simply too wonderful and too universally appealing to restrict to an arbitrary framework. Accordingly, I have brought them together in this chapter, rightly named "Good Stuff Whenever You Can Get It" and called "Good Stuff" for short: all those foods you remember so fondly from grandmother's house (if you are fifty or above and which you are likely to have missed altogether if you are forty or below).

Into even the hardest life some hot bread and butter must fall. A better life includes some cake, too, and the best lives get some lemon pie as well. Let's hope for a good life and enjoy the food.

I can remember some fairly bleak times in my life, but I cannot remember a time so bleak that we did not have desserts. At Mammy Dossett's there was always something—pie or cake or bread pudding or custard. These desserts were never fancy, but they were good. At the Weavers' it was no different. When we moved away from my grandmother's, my mother continued the practice. A meal might not have meat, but it had dessert. It probably had bread. And it was good stuff.

I need to tell you a couple of things to help you understand some of the dessert recipes that will follow shortly. You shouldn't be surprised to find a number of ingredients that at first glance don't quite fit with the sort of country living I've been telling you about. The heavy use of flavoring extracts is a good example. We had ready access, however, to ingredients of that sort through a kind of enterprise that flourished then but has all but disappeared now—the door-to-door salesman. The Watkins' man was a regular. From him we bought vanilla, lemon, and even maple extract. We also bought salve and liniment and other essentials.

Of course, somebody in the neighborhood was always selling Cloverleaf Salve. Mammy Dossett bought some once just because I wanted one of the pictures you were given if you bought a can. I chose one of a boy arriving home with all the obvious marks of having been in a fight. His mother is so astounded at the sight of him that she has dropped a pie. The cat, about to be hit by the falling pie, stands with its back arched and its tail in the air. I know the details of this picture so well because we sat down that very afternoon and arranged the cloverleaf salve picture with a group of family pictures over an old print of some sort that hung in the dining room. This collection of pictures, now rather faded and dingy, still hangs in my office at home.

When I was growing up, there were hot biscuits every morning and hot cornbread for dinner. There might be light bread, and there might even be rolls. There were always biscuits. For many years, biscuits were surrounded by an air of mystery. A story circulated that they were somehow difficult to make (untrue!), and jokes about killing the dog with a new bride's biscuits became part of common lore. Then biscuits were rediscovered, and they were suddenly everywhere. The Colonel made you take them whether you wanted them or not, and everybody started selling "breakfast biscuits"—strange objects with anonymous fillings and paper wrappers. It's a shame that most biscuits served in fast-food places today are so bad; in my humble opinion, there is no reason not to make *good* biscuits.

To be really good, biscuits must have some body and they

must have a subtle taste. Most modern biscuits fail on both counts. They are so filled with artificial leavening agents that all you taste is baking powder and all you get is crumbs in the lap and grease on the fingers. Let's get to the real heart of the matter. Good biscuits are a combination of flour, shortening, salt, milk, and something to make them rise. They are made from a reasonably soft and fairly sticky dough which is kneaded very little. But this basic formula encompasses all sorts of variants.

My Mammy Dossett made soda biscuits. She shaped them by hand and baked them close together on a black steel pan in a hot oven. They were sometimes called "Cat Heads" (probably because of their size and shape). She made these biscuits in a big pan which was filled with flour and kept in the flour drawer of a big old-fashioned kitchen cabinet. She measured nothing. She made a well in the center of a panful of flour and poured some buttermilk into it. She added a hunk of lard, some salt, and some baking soda. She worked enough flour into the milk to make a dough of the proper consistency, and while she was doing this, she blended the lard into it. She would knead the dough lightly a few times in the remaining flour and start to make out the biscuits. She pinched off a piece of dough (always the same size!), rolled it between her hands, flattened it, and placed it on the greased pan. She then did the next and the next until the pan was just filled with biscuits of matching shape and size. It was routine. Today, my mother can and does make them the same way. Although I have tried this method, I am not expert at it. Furthermore, it is not worth the effort. I roll them, I cut them, I bake them, and I eat them. But I remember the way she did it.

Soda biscuits are generally not light enough or flaky enough for today's taste, but they are good to bake on the top of a chicken casserole or to knead a little more and roll to make pie dough. Someday when you are having country-fried steak and want something to stand up to the gravy, try soda biscuits.

Soda Biscuits

2 cups all-purpose flour
⅓ cup shortening
¾ cup buttermilk

½ teaspoon salt
1½ teaspoon baking soda

Add the salt and the soda to the flour and blend well. Work in the shortening until the mixture resembles coarse cornmeal. Add the milk and stir to make a reasonably soft dough. Turn out onto a heavily floured board and knead lightly 5 or 6 times or until the surface is just smooth. Roll or pat out until about ½ inch thick and cut with a biscuit cutter. Rework, reroll, and cut the scrap until all the dough has been used. Place on a lightly greased cookie sheet with the sides touching. If you use a 2½-inch cutter this will make about a dozen biscuits. Bake in a 400° oven until brown (about 15 minutes).

You will find that many old cookbooks talk about **cream of tartar biscuits**. If you want to give them a try, do so as a variation on soda biscuits. Simply make the biscuits above, reducing the soda to 1 teaspoon and add about 2 teaspoons of cream of tartar as well. If your buttermilk is not very sour, you may notice a slight yellow color in your biscuits. In the classic East Tennessee kitchen, that would have been a flaw in the bread, but not a fatal one. The basic rule is 1 teaspoon soda for each cup of buttermilk, but that makes biscuits too heavy even for me. If anybody questions the color, tell them it is because you use a special kind of flour. Who will know?

Before we go on with variations on the biscuit theme, let me establish a couple of ground rules for you. All these recipes will be based on 2 cups of flour. They are easy to double, triple, or otherwise multiply however you choose. I generally use a 2½-inch cutter for everyday biscuits, and that will be the standard if I give numbers. Remember that this is an art and not a science. Be brave! Experiment for yourself. For example, if I am going to use biscuits with country ham on a buffet, I roll the dough to about a quarter of an inch thick and cut out the biscuits with a delightful little 1-inch cutter which someone gave me. This produces a thin, bite-sized, crusty biscuit which is perfect with a sliver of baked country ham.

Today's taste is probably best served by buttermilk biscuits, which use both soda and baking powder. This is my customary way of making biscuits.

Buttermilk Biscuits

2 cups all-purpose flour

½ teaspoon salt

⅓ cup shortening

1 teaspoon baking soda

¾ cup buttermilk

2 teaspoons baking powder

Mix together the dry ingredients and work in the shortening until it is well blended. Stir in the milk to make a soft dough. Turn out onto a heavily floured board and knead a few times. Roll or pat to about ½ inch thick. Cut with a biscuit cutter and place on a lightly greased cookie sheet with adjacent biscuits touching. Continue to rework and reroll the dough until it all has been cut. Bake in a 400° oven until the biscuits are brown.

If you don't have buttermilk available, you have two alternatives. (You really have three if you include borrowing some from your neighbor, but surely you understand that.) You can make an acceptable buttermilk for cooking by adding 2 or 3 tablespoons white vinegar to a cup of milk (you can use cider vinegar, but you will be able to taste it). Or you can make the biscuits with sweet milk by simply leaving out the soda and increasing the baking powder to 1 tablespoon. They are better with buttermilk, though.

If you're perpetually in a hurry and won't tell anyone that I was the one who told you, I'll let you in on a biscuit secret: You can make perfectly acceptable biscuits using cooking oil. Let's call these

Secret Biscuits

2 cups flour	½ teaspoon salt
⅓ cup cooking oil	1 tablespoon baking powder
⅔ cup milk	

Thoroughly mix all the ingredients. Shape into a ball and pat or roll on a piece of waxed paper to ½ inch thick and cut into biscuits. Rework and reroll the dough to use it all. Bake on a cookie sheet with the edges touching in a 400° oven until brown. This dough is not sticky at all—great to handle.

In case you wonder, that business about baking biscuits with the edges touching is a matter of choice. If baked this way, biscuits rise higher and have soft sides. If you like biscuits to have more crust and less center, roll the dough thinner and place the biscuits on the pan so the sides do not touch. While we are talking about biscuits in general, I ought to say something about self-rising flour. This is simply flour to which salt and baking powder have already been added. It is fine for making biscuits if you do it all the time and like this extra convenience. Since self-rising flour cannot be used in many other things and because I see no reason to bother with two kinds of flour, I don't use it. And if you will pardon one small chauvinistic addition (Knoxville chauvinism, not male chauvinism), I do find that Knoxville's White Lily flour with its high soft wheat content is best for biscuits.

The queen of biscuits, of course, was the one which was raised at least in part with yeast. Such a biscuit was a special treat because yeast was not all that common in East Tennessee. While many families kept a yeast growing, we were not that cultured. In my early life, yeast came from the grocery store in Knoxville. It was kept cool and usually worked but not always. Therefore, yeast biscuits, which were called "riz biscuits" in my neighborhood, were looked on as a real treat. Many old books call them "angel biscuits" because they were as soft as an angel's wing. Whatever they were called, they were, and are, good. The following recipe is an old one and, therefore, calls for much larger amounts than the other recipes I have given you. This is not a problem. Everyone will want more of these.

Angel Biscuits

5 cups all-purpose flour

1 cup shortening

1 teaspoon soda

1 tablespoon baking
    powder

1 tablespoon sugar

1 teaspoon salt

1 package dry yeast

¼ cup lukewarm water

1¾ cups buttermilk

Dissolve the yeast in the warm water. In another bowl, blend the dry ingredients, then work the shortening in thoroughly. Add the yeast mixture and the buttermilk and stir together to make a soft dough. Knead just enough to hold together. Roll to preferred thickness (¼ to ½ inch) and place on a cookie sheet. Bake in a 400° oven until biscuits are brown (about 20 minutes).

As I've said before, biscuit dough can be used for other things, such as pie crust. Here's another use I might as well mention now: "Stickies," as they were called in our house. These little delights are a prime example of how to make the best of what you have.

Stickies

2 cups flour	1 tablespoon baking powder
⅓ cup shortening	¼ cup butter, softened
¾ cup milk	1 cup sugar (white or brown)
1 teaspoon salt	1 tablespoon ground cinnamon

Mix the flour, salt, and baking powder. Blend in the shortening. Add the milk and stir to make a soft dough. Turn out onto a heavily floured board and knead in enough flour to make a stiff, easily rolled dough. Roll about ⅛ inch thick. Spread with the softened butter and sprinkle on half of the sugar and cinnamon, which have been mixed together. Roll up jelly-roll fashion and cut crosswise about ¼ inch thick. Place cut side down in a buttered 9-by-13-by-2-inch pan into which the remaining sugar and cinnamon have been spread. When all the rolls are in place, pour 1 cup water over them and place immediately into a 375° oven and bake about 30 minutes or until brown. Serve warm, spooning the rolls out onto a plate and the syrup which will have formed in the bottom of the pan onto them. If you are feeling particularly decadent, top them with a little whipped cream.

As universal as biscuits and just as good in its own way is cornbread. The trick is to find good cornmeal. Many folks were not interested in any cornmeal that was not from corn they themselves had grown. I can well remember going with my Great-grandpa Weaver to a mill somewhere in Union County to have corn ground "on the shares": That is, the miller kept part of the meal as his fee for grinding the corn rather than receiving a cash payment. I believe this mill was somewhere in the Sharp's Chapel section of Union County, but I'm not sure about that. I do remember someone at the mill taking me to the mill race and showing me how you stopped the mill by inserting a board in the race to divert the water. In later years, as we Americans struggled with the energy crisis, I remembered that elementary lesson in the uses of natural energy.

There are still some mills scattered through East Tennessee where you can get fresh water-ground meal, and I have been pleased to see them prosper in recent years and some idle ones reopen. Creditable cornbread can be made from the current cornmeal mixes on the market. However, cornbread will never be as good as when you make it from meal and can control all the other ingredients. If you live in East Tennessee or travel through here, you can turn a trip to buy good meal into a wonderful afternoon by visiting the Crosseyed Cricket. This delightful catfish restaurant, which is located just off I-40 in the Lenoir City area, is in an old mill building. They have installed a modern gristmill, selling white and yellow cornmeal as well as whole wheat flour. Take the kids, catch your dinner, and take home some meal. Good mills also operate in Pigeon Forge and Norris. Within the past couple of years, Teague Mill has opened near Pittman Center outside of Gatlinburg. It, too, has a delightful restaurant as well as an operating mill that produces whole wheat flour and cornmeal.

I'll have to admit I'm not totally unprejudiced on the subject of cornbread. First, I was raised to believe that only poor people ate yellow cornmeal. Therefore, to ensure that no one could think we were poor, we didn't eat it. Second, I was raised to believe that the adding of eggs, sugar, or other adulterants to good everyday cornbread was the sort of thing that started Rome toward its fall. We didn't do it. Corn sticks and muffins were suspect but didn't automatically damn you. My upbringing is one of the reasons that I set spoon bread off in another section of the book. I love it, but I have learned to since I was an adult. We didn't have it at home. We had cornbread.

Traditional Cornbread

2 cups plain cornmeal

1 cup plain flour

2 teaspoons soda

1 teaspoon salt

2 cups buttermilk

Mix together the dry ingredients. Stir in the buttermilk. The batter should be too thin to hold its shape. Pour into a heavily greased, well-seasoned #8 (10-inch) cast-iron skillet. Bake in a 425° oven until brown (about 30 minutes).

Note. This recipe will produce a fairly heavy bread. If you want to lighten it a little, add 2 teaspoons baking powder. That is the way I usually make cornbread.

I should also tell you I have a skillet which is reserved for baking cornbread. It is used for nothing else and is washed only with hot water. No soap has touched it in years, and for someone to mess with it now would provoke me to wrath so great that I cannot begin to describe it. This is because cornbread has a tendency to stick and nothing removes the seasoning from a cast-iron skillet as much as soap. If the seasoning is removed, the bread sticks—the flavor is not impaired, but the appearance assuredly is. The proper pan to use for cornbread is itself the subject of debate reaching legendary proportions. While my mother's family used an iron skillet, my father's family used a flat, black steel pan. The skillet produces a heavier crust and I prefer it. However, there are some good black steel pans coming on the market today, and you might want to try one. Remember to grease the pan heavily. The recipe above should be baked in an 8-inch pan if you like thick cornbread but can be baked in a larger pan if you prefer it thinner and crustier.

Most cornmeal today is sold as a mix which already has the flour, baking powder, and salt added. This mix makes a reasonably good, traditional cornbread if you use 3 cups of the mix with 2 cups of regular milk. (If you use buttermilk, be sure to add 1 teaspoon soda for each cup of buttermilk.) Proceed to bake as above. I don't like the mix so well because the corn is ground much finer than was traditional and therefore produces a bread with less texture. But I must admit that it is convenient, so I use it often.

I have been instructed by my wife not to allow my prejudices to spoil your pleasure in a number of fancier cornbreads. They follow. She's a city girl, and she'll have to take the blame if these recipes lead to further decay of traditional values in this country.

Fancy Cornbread

2 cups self-rising cornmeal mix (white or yellow)

3 tablespoons sugar

2 eggs, lightly beaten

1 cup milk

¼ cup melted shortening or cooking oil

Mix all the ingredients and bake as either corn muffins, corn sticks, or cornbread. Remember to use well-greased pans and bake in a 425° oven until brown.

To help redeem ourselves, let's talk about something more traditional:

Fried Cornbread

2 cups cornmeal	1 teaspoon salt
½ cup flour	1½ to 2 cups hot water
1 tablespoon baking powder	bacon grease for frying

Mix the dry ingredients and stir in enough hot water to make a batter about the consistency of pancake batter. Heat a flat griddle (preferably well-seasoned cast-iron) and grease generously with salt-bacon grease. If you have no salt bacon grease, use commercial. If you have no commercial bacon grease, use shortening. The cornbread won't be as good but will be, therefore, healthier. (The nutritionists should be pacified.) Pour the cornmeal batter onto the griddle to make cakes about 3 inches across. Fry until brown on the bottom and starting to look bubbly around the edges. Turn and brown on the other side. After pre-heating the griddle, you should use about medium heat or the corn cakes will brown before they have cooked through. Continue to regrease the griddle between each frying and continue to fry until all the batter has been used. The batter will need to be stirred regularly while using. Serve hot.

One wonderfully traditional use of cornmeal in Middle Tennessee was unknown to me as an East Tennessee child, but I think it is delicious. This recipe is a old one from the family of Phila Rawlings Hach. Phila (probably the best-known person in food circles in Tennessee) has written a half-dozen wonderful cookbooks and operates Hachland Hill Dining Inn in Clarksville, Tennessee. Look for her cookbooks. And if you are ever in that area, call to see if you can get a reservation at Hachland Hill (you won't get in otherwise).

Corn Light Bread

3 cups cornmeal	1 tablespoon shortening (or lard)
1 cup flour	1 package dry yeast
1 tablespoon sugar	3 cups milk
1 teaspoon salt	3 eggs

Mix the dry ingredients and work in the shortening until it is fully blended. Stir in the eggs. Heat the milk until it is lukewarm and stir in the yeast until it is dissolved. Stir the milk into the meal mixture to make a stiff batter. Pour into 2 well-greased 8-inch cake pans or 2 well-greased 9-by-5-by-3-inch loaf pans. Cover and allow to rise in a warm place until the batter rises (about 1½ hours.) Bake in a preheated 350° oven until the bread is brown. This will take about 45 minutes in the cake pans and a little longer in loaf pans. Serve hot with butter.

Earlier we talked about **cracklin' bread**. Remember, you can use any of the cornbread recipes (I prefer the traditional one). Just stir in about a cup of good cracklings and bake as usual. And don't forget about cornmeal mush and spoon bread just because we talked about them back in "Fall."

Before we leave cornbread, we need to talk about a food phenomenon in East Tennessee that must be experienced to be understood. I cannot explain the appeal of cornbread and milk to anyone. I simply know that the real reason to make cornbread is to have some left over so it can be eaten cold, crumbled into milk. Some people think that this can be done only with buttermilk. Others think any kind of milk will do. I personally hold with the idea that it must be cold sweet milk. Whatever your choice of milk is, you can return with me now to those delightful days of yesteryear when an integral part of supper was cold cornbread crumbled into a large glass or a bowl and cold milk poured over it. It should be eaten immediately while the crust is still crisp and the inside of the bread has some character.

Hush puppies are also worth a mention. As you probably

know, these little pieces of fried cornbread were made to serve with fried fish. To make hush puppies, simply use your favorite of the cornbreads above, reducing the liquid by about one-fourth to make a stiff batter. Stir in a very finely chopped onion (I like thinly sliced green onion, about ¼ cup for 4 cups of batter) and blend it in. Drop the batter by teaspoonfuls into hot deep fat and fry until brown. Drain and serve with fish. You may also want to slice some potatoes and deep fry them in the same fat. Not only will that allow you to indulge yourself, but it will also remove the last of the fish taste from the fat.

As seldom as I saw yeast bread as a child, I love it too much not to include it here. I believe my deprivation was a fairly typical one for the time and place. Yeast was simply not readily available way out in the country where we lived—after all, it was eighteen miles to town. For the historical record, though, I'll have to admit that I've seen a large section on yeast bread in a cookbook published in Knoxville in 1900. While a few of the recipes in this cookbook talked about home-grown yeast, most simply instructed the reader to "take a cake of Fleishmann's Yeast." That's traditional enough for me.

Yeast Bread

2 cups liquid (milk, water, or cream)   1 package dry yeast
3 tablespoons shortening   ¼ cup warm water
3 tablespoons sugar   4 to 5 cups flour
2 teaspoons salt

Heat the liquid with the shortening, sugar, and salt until the shortening is melted. Remove from the heat and allow to cool to lukewarm. While this is cooling, dissolve the yeast in ¼ cup lukewarm water. When the liquid is lukewarm, add the yeast and 1 cup flour and stir thoroughly to make a batter. Cover and allow to rise in a warm place at least 1 hour or until bubbly. Beat in enough flour to make a stiff dough. Turn the dough out onto a heavily floured board and knead until smooth.

Place in a greased bowl and turn to grease all sides of the dough. Cover and allow to rise until doubled in bulk. Punch down and shape into one large or two regular sized loaves. Place into loaf pans of an appropriate size (one 9-by-5-by-3-inch or two 8-by-5-by-2½-inch) and allow to rise again. Bake in a 325° oven about 45 minutes or until the bread is brown. When done, the bread will have a hollow sound when tapped.

I won't let my personal deprivation color this book entirely. My family seldom had rolls. Although I love them, I almost never make them because I'm not very good at it. A friend has supplied this recipe.

Hot Rolls

2 cups milk

½ cup shortening

½ cup sugar

1 package dry yeast

½ teaspoon soda

1 teaspoon baking powder

1 teaspoon salt

6 cups flour

melted butter

Scald the milk and add the shortening and sugar. Allow to cool to lukewarm. Remove ¼ cup of the warm milk mixture and dissolve the yeast in it. Return it to the warm milk. Put 4 cups of the flour in a large mixing bowl. Pour the milk and yeast mixture over it and beat well. Allow to rise in a warm place until double in bulk. Beat down and add the soda, baking powder, salt, and enough of the remaining flour to make a soft dough. Knead lightly and shape as desired. Dip the rolls in butter and allow them to rise in a shallow pan until double in bulk. Bake in a 450° oven until the rolls are brown.

This recipe works nicely for **Parker House rolls**. Simply roll the dough, cut it with a biscuit cutter, and fold each roll in half after dipping it in the butter. They also do very well as **cloverleaf rolls**. For these, roll small pieces of the dough lightly into balls and dip each one in butter. Place three or four of the balls into a muffin tin and allow to rise before baking.

Now let's turn to what you really wanted to know in the first place. What's for dessert? It might be cake or pie or bread pudding or even chocolate pudding. It might be fruit pies or cream pies or custard pies. There was almost always something. You might say dessert was our chief extravagance. My mother's family had very little money, but they kept a box of cornstarch in the kitchen exclusively for making lemon pie. They viewed buying lemons as decadent, and you can imagine how they felt about buying cornstarch just so the filling would look better. But they did it anyway.

Most often, pies meant fruit cobblers. Remember, this is a cuisine designed to make the most of what you had. You could buy a fifty-pound bag of sugar very cheaply. You grew the fruit or picked it wild. It was a natural. In "Fall" we talked about apples and apple pie. Now we need to talk about pie crusts, which my great-grandmother taught me were, like promises, made to be broken.

In our household, two kinds of pie crusts were usual. For everyday cobblers, the crust was simply biscuit dough which was kneaded a little and rolled thin to line a deep cobbler pan and cover most of the top of the fruit filling. In case you don't know, a cobbler is a kind of deep-dish pie. You make a simple pie crust, roll it thin, and line a pan about 2 inches deep. Then you fill it with fruit, sugar, and a little butter, cover the top with another pie crust, and bake it. You eat it hot or cold. You eat it with cream, whipped cream, butter, cheese, ice cream, or simply by itself. Its simplicity is its greatness. The fact that you can taste the fruit doesn't hurt. On the other hand, pastry—made with lard, seldom with butter—was used for either fruit or other pies, both single- and double-crust. The two basic recipes follow. Remember that I am giving you the *traditional* way of doing this and not necessarily what is the *best* way. I still use the biscuit-like dough for cobblers because it changes both the taste and consistency to use regular pastry. For pies, I often do an old-fashioned shortening pastry if

I'm in a hurry. I like the taste of butter pastry or some of the modern cream cheese pastries better, but they take longer, are more temperamental, and sometimes fail. An old-fashioned lard pastry (made with Crisco or some other good-quality shortening) never does.

Pie Crust for Cobblers

2 cups plain flour

1 teaspoon salt

1 tablespoon baking powder

⅓ cup shortening

¾ cup milk

Mix the dry ingredients and work in the shortening until the mixture resembles cornmeal. Add the milk and work the mixture into a light dough. Turn out onto a heavily floured board and knead until smooth. Roll until very thin. Line an 8-by-8-inch pan with the dough, using the trimmings to cover the top after the fruit filling has been added. A cobbler should be baked in the center of a 350° oven until the top crust is brown. This will take about 45 minutes.

Shortening Pastry

1 cup plain flour

½ teaspoon salt

½ teaspoon baking powder

⅓ cup solid shortening

3 tablespoons cold water
   (approximately)

Mix together the dry ingredients and work in the shortening. Add the cold water and work into a firm dough. Add extra water if necessary to get the pastry to hold together. Shape the pastry into a flat ball and roll on a lightly floured board until thin. This is enough to line an 8- or 9-inch pie pan. Double the recipe for a two-crust pie.

   Note: If you prefer, you may use butter instead of the shortening. If you do use butter, work it in quickly. Shape the pastry into a ball, wrap it with wax paper, aluminum foil, or plastic wrap, and allow it to chill a couple of hours before you roll it. (See why I prefer to make pastry with shortening?)

We have talked about some pies as we moved through the year. (Remember the index.) The following fillings are all to be used with an 8-inch cobbler. By now, you must know that I selected that size and amount arbitrarily. My mother, cooking for the hordes that moved through our house, made cobbler in a huge pan. Once you have mastered the idea from these recipes, you simply double or triple the ingredients to get the size of cobbler you need. With many recipes, you can't do that. All sorts of subtle things like the amount of top space of the pan and baking times intervene. Not so with cobblers.

In addition to the fruit fillings mentioned before, here are two others that are also very good.

Peach Cobbler

| 3 cups sliced peaches | ¾ cup sugar | 4 tablespoons butter |

Line a cobbler pan with pie dough (see p. 175) and put in the sliced fresh peaches. Sprinkle with the sugar and the butter cut into small pieces. Cover the top with dough and bake at 350° until brown (about 45 minutes).

Note. This recipe can also be done with canned peaches. If the peaches are canned in heavy syrup, simply add the butter and about 2 tablespoons flour to the peaches and juice. Blend the flour in thoroughly and bring the peach mixture to a boil before pouring it into the pie crust.

Cherry Cobbler

| 4 cups sour cherries | 1 cup sugar | 4 tablespoons butter |

Pit the cherries and mix with the sugar. Bring to a boil before pouring into the pie crust (see p. 175). Cut the butter into small pieces on top of the fruit, cover with the top crust, and bake in a 350° oven until brown.

I can't leave cobblers without mentioning a special kind. No country garden was complete without rhubarb. This beautiful perennial was grown for the stems of the leaves. (The leaves were not eaten, only the stems.) The bright red or green stems were cut crosswise, cooked with a lot of sugar (they are very sour) and made into pies either on their own or mixed with strawberries. Rhubarb is now enjoying a resurgence of popularity, and I recommend it to you. When I was growing up, Granny Weaver had several rhubarb plants which grew at the end of the garden along the fence. I can remember going with her in the early spring to see if the strange little round balls which herald the new growth of rhubarb had pushed through the ground. Rhubarb makes an attractive addition to a sunny corner of a flower bed. Most mail order seed and gardening supply houses sell the roots, and once established, it will grow forever. You can sometimes find the stems already pulled and the leaves cut off in the grocery stores.

Strawberry-Rhubarb Cobbler

2 cups fresh rhubarb	2 cups strawberries
1½ cups sugar	4 tablespoons butter

Cap the strawberries, cut into halves, and set aside. Cut the rhubarb crosswise into ½-inch-long pieces. Put the rhubarb and the sugar into a heavy saucepan with a couple of tablespoons of water and bring it slowly to a boil, stirring occasionally. When the rhubarb mixture boils, remove from the heat, stir in the strawberries, and pour into the cobbler crust (see p. 175). Cover with a top crust and bake at 350° until brown.

Converting any of these cobbler fillings to a more sophisticated **double-crust fruit pie** is very simple. When you prepare your filling, simply add about 2 tablespoons flour or cornstarch to the mixture and blend it thoroughly before cooking the filling. Make enough of the shortening pastry (see p. 175) for a double-crust pie and proceed.

One of the charms of a cobbler is the natural juices that form and are only slightly thickened by the flour from the crust. But as you can see, I prefer the filling of a regular pie to be thicker than that of a cobbler. (While we're on fruit pies, don't forget those apple, blackberry, grape, and green tomato ones that we talked about back in "Summer" and "Fall.")

Pies were not necessarily *fruit* pies. Remember that milk and cream were readily available, as were eggs. With those ingredients around, what could be a more natural outcome than various custard and cream pies? Probably the best known of the traditional custard pies was chess pie.

Chess Pie

1 cup sugar

6 tablespoons butter,
   melted and cooled

2 tablespoons flour

2 tablespoons cornmeal

3 eggs

1 cup milk

1 teaspoon vanilla

½ teaspoon lemon extract

Mix the sugar, flour, and cornmeal. Beat in the eggs, one at a time. Stir in the melted butter. Add the milk slowly until fully blended, then the vanilla. Pour into an unbaked 9-inch pastry shell (see p. 175) and bake in a 350° oven for 40 minutes or until a knife inserted in the center comes out clean.

If you want a treat which is nontraditional but good, stir about ¼ cup cocoa into the sugar mixture and have **chocolate chess pie**.

A more traditional variation on chess pie, and one I think I like even better, is

Buttermilk Pie

1 cup sugar	3 eggs
¼ pound butter, melted and cooled	1 cup buttermilk
4 tablespoons flour	1 tablespoon lemon extract

Mix sugar and flour. Beat in eggs one at a time and then beat in the butter. Stir the milk in slowly to blend fully, then the lemon extract. Pour into an unbaked 9-inch pie shell (see p. 175) and bake at 350° until done (about 45 minutes).

If you like **coconut custard pie,** simply make a buttermilk pie and stir in about ½ cup flaked coconut with the lemon. Bake as usual. It is delightful.

In my own personal history, no pie ranks so high as egg custard. I know egg custard pie is bland, but it represents all the good things of childhood to me. Egg custard is easy enough to make. Let me know if you keep the bottom crust from becoming soggy—that is the ultimate test of a good custard pie. If that is important to you, in making custard pies or any other pie that cooks in the shell, partly precook the shell by lining it with waxed paper, filling it with rice or dried beans to hold it in shape, and then baking it on a middle or lower rack in a 350° oven for about 10 minutes. Remove the weights and the paper while the crust is still hot and brush the hot crust with beaten egg. (If you are making a prebaked crust for another purpose, simply remove the weights and the paper and return the crust to the oven for about another 10 minutes or until the crust is lightly browned.)

Egg Custard Pie

2 cups milk	1 tablespoon flour
3 eggs	1 tablespoon vanilla
½ cup sugar	nutmeg

Mix together the sugar and flour. Beat in the eggs and slowly stir in the milk to blend smoothly. Add the vanilla and pour into a partially baked 9-inch pastry (see p. 175). Sprinkle the top with ground nutmeg. Bake in a 350° oven until set and lightly browned (about 45 minutes).

One of the strangest pies I know of is vinegar pie. When I asked my mother how anyone ever came up with something like this in the first place, she reminded me that by the end of February, when you might be scraping the bottom of the barrel, just about any kind of pie seemed good. I have to admit that for something so unlikely sounding, it's not that bad. The basic recipe for the two that follow is one I found among my Grandmother Freeman's things after she had died. My mother and I argue about what kind of pie she made with this filling—custard or meringue? I still believe the custard is more authentic.

Vinegar Custard Pie

2 tablespoons butter	2 eggs
½ cup sugar	2 tablespoons cider vinegar
3 tablespoons flour	1 cup water
¼ teaspoon salt	

Mix the flour, sugar, and salt. Beat in the eggs and stir in the melted butter. Beat in the vinegar and water and mix thoroughly. Pour into an unbaked 8-inch pastry shell (see p. 175) and bake at 350° until set.

The other recipe is slightly more sophisticated (if any dessert of this simplicity deserves that term). It makes use of exactly the same ingredients cooked another way.

Vinegar Meringue Pie

2 tablespoons butter

½ cup sugar

3 tablespoons flour

¼ teaspoon salt

2 eggs

2 tablespoons vinegar

1 cup water

Mix together the sugar, flour, and salt in a heavy saucepan. Beat in the two egg yolks. Slowly beat in the water and the vinegar, mixing thoroughly. Place on medium heat, stirring constantly until the mixture comes to a full boil and is thick. Stir in the butter. Pour into a prebaked 8-inch pie shell. Beat the two egg whites until frothy and then beat in 6 tablespoons sugar and continue beating until stiff peaks form. Spread the meringue on the cooled pie filling, sealing to the edges. Bake in a 350° oven until lightly brown (about 12 to 15 minutes.) Serve cool.

In discussing pies, I've saved for last what I consider to be the real cream of pies. Whether chocolate, lemon, coconut or butterscotch, these cream pies are wonderful. Lemon is my favorite. As I hinted earlier, if you want to have a really clear lemon filling, you must make it with cornstarch. But suit yourself—it *tastes* just as good with flour. I like lemon pie made with fresh lemon juice, but in the old days it was much more usual to flavor it with lemon extract.

Lemon Pie

1¾ cups sugar

4 tablespoons cornstarch
   (or flour)

¼ teaspoon salt

1½ cups water

3 eggs, separated

2 tablespoons butter

½ teaspoon grated lemon
   peel (optional)

⅓ cup lemon juice (or
   1 tablespoon lemon extract)

¼ teaspoon cream of tartar

1 9-inch baked pie shell
   (see p. 175)

Mix 1½ cups of the sugar, the cornstarch, and the salt in a heavy sauce-pan. Stir in the water. Mix well. Bring to a boil, stirring constantly. Stir a small amount of the hot mixture into the beaten egg yolks and stir the yolks back into the hot mixture in the pan. Return to a boil and cook about 1 minute. Remove from the heat and stir in the butter and the lemon juice and lemon peel (or the lemon extract). Bring just back to a boil; then remove from the heat, pour into the baked pie shell, and allow to cool. While the filling is cooling, beat the egg whites until frothy; add the cream of tartar and the remaining ¼ cup sugar and continue beating until stiff peaks form. Spread the meringue over the cooled lemon filling, sealing it to the edges of the pie. Bake in a 350° oven until the meringue is lightly brown. Serve cold.

Chocolate Pie

1¼ cups sugar

2 tablespoons flour

¼ teaspoon salt

⅓ cup cocoa

3 eggs, separated

2 cups milk

¼ teaspoon cream of tartar

1 8- or 9-inch prebaked pie
   shell (see p. 175)

Mix 1 cup sugar, the flour, salt, and cocoa together in a heavy saucepan. Beat in the egg yolks and slowly beat in the milk until thoroughly mixed. Place on medium heat and cook, stirring constantly until boiling and thick. Remove from the heat and pour into the baked pie shell. Beat the egg whites until frothy and beat in the cream of tartar and the ¼ cup sugar. Continue to beat until stiff peaks form. Spread the meringue over the cooled filling, being sure to seal to the edges. Bake in a preheated 350° oven until lightly brown. Serve cool.

A whole series of variations is possible with the basic meringue pie recipe, which I just gave you in the chocolate version. If you want **coconut pie,** simply leave out the cocoa and cook as directed; then stir in 1 teaspoon vanilla and ½ cup shredded or flaked coconut. Sprinkle more coconut on the top of the pie before browning it. For **pineapple pie,** substitute drained, crushed pineapple for the coconut.

A passable **butterscotch pie** can be made by using brown sugar rather than the white. I should tell you, however, that this is not the traditional way to make butterscotch pie. In that wonderful concoction, one-half of the sugar was caramelized in a heavy pan and stirred back into the custard when it finished cooking while both were very hot. If you decide to try this, simply place half of the sugar in a heavy pan on medium heat and stir it until it melts and becomes lightly browned. Be careful! It burns very easily. Keep this melted sugar just hot enough to stay melted while you prepare the pie filling. Then stir the hot, caramalized sugar into the boiling filling, blending it thoroughly. Pour it into a baked pie shell and proceed with the meringue.

When you didn't want to go to the trouble of making pastry, you could always have pudding for dessert. Pudding is a particularly good example of how we used readily available ingredients to their best advantage: all you needed to buy was some sugar and a little Watkins Extract and you could make a good dessert. The most traditional of these puddings was simply boiled custard. Here are a couple of traditional ways to make it—you can decide which you like better.

Egg Custard I

3 eggs   1 tablespoon vanilla

2½ cups milk   nutmeg

½ cup sugar

Beat the eggs and mix with the sugar. Stir in the milk. Put into the top of a double boiler and cook over boiling water until thick. Stir in the vanilla. Serve cold with nutmeg sprinkled on the top.

Egg Custard II

4 eggs, separated   1 tablespoon vanilla

3 cups milk   nutmeg

¾ cup sugar

Separate the eggs and beat the egg whites with ¼ cup sugar until stiff. Blend the egg yolks and the remaining sugar and stir in the milk. Cook in the top of a double boiler over boiling water until thick. Blend a small amount of the hot custard into the egg whites to warm them and then fold the egg white mixture into the hot custard. Spoon out into serving dishes and cool. Sprinkle with nutmeg and serve.

It seems appropriate to me to say a word about this apparently simple dessert. For some reason that I do not understand, the story has grown that boiled custard is somehow difficult to make—especially that it is hard to make without lumps. But I've never had this problem: I make it in a double boiler and stir it constantly. However, I also know that if it should lump, those lumps can be reincorporated into the custard by beating it strongly with a French whisk while it is still warm. By the way, did I mention that it is important in making custard and any other delicate dish in a double boiler that the water not touch the upper pan? Consider yourself told.

Probably even more common than egg custard were flour puddings. These puddings start with basically the same mixture as for custard, but with flour added to make the pudding stiffer.

(Flour also made it even easier to make.) I will give you the basic flour pudding and then several variations on it. It makes as good a dessert today as it did when I was growing up.

Vanilla Pudding

3 eggs	4 tablespoons flour
4 cups milk	1 tablespoon vanilla
1½ cups sugar	

In a heavy saucepan, blend together the sugar and the flour. Beat in the eggs. Stir in the milk and place the mixture over medium heat. Stir constantly until the pudding comes to a boil and is thick. Remove from heat and stir in the vanilla. Serve cold.

This mixture lends itself to variations. The most common are chocolate and butterscotch pudding. For **chocolate pudding,** simply stir ½ cup good cocoa in with the sugar and flour and proceed as usual. I sometimes leave the vanilla in, and I sometimes leave it out; you can see for yourself which way you prefer. For **butterscotch pudding,** simply use brown sugar instead of white.

Vanilla pudding is also the basis for one of the real treats of this region and one of life's genuine joys—banana pudding. Unfortunately, this is another one of those foods which is simple to make but is usually made poorly. People who tell you that they can do it just as well as Grandma did but use instant pudding and leave off the meringue either had a poor cook for a grandmother or they will lie about other things, too. *Real* banana pudding is made with vanilla wafers, good ripe bananas, and vanilla pudding, then topped with meringue and browned. It is served at room temperature, and you don't have to worry about it spoiling—it won't last that long. Seriously, it doesn't keep well and, in my opinion, isn't very good when it stands for a long time in the refrigerator. So serve it when you have friends over and eat the whole thing.

Banana Pudding

6 eggs, separated

4 cups milk

1½ cups sugar

4 tablespoons flour

1 tablespoon vanilla

Separate the eggs and reserve the whites for meringue. Stir 1¼ cups of the sugar and the flour together. Beat in the egg yolks until completely blended. Stir in the milk. Cook over medium heat until the mixture boils and is thick. Stir in the vanilla. Set aside to cool. While the pudding is cooling, peel and slice 5 bananas crosswise. Place a layer of vanilla wafers to cover the bottom of a 2-quart heatproof dish. Cover with a layer of banana slices and cover the bananas with a layer of the warm pudding. Repeat with layers of vanilla wafers, bananas, and pudding until the dish is full.

Beat the egg whites until frothy and then add the cream of tartar and the reserved ¼ cup sugar slowly while continuing to beat them. When the meringue is stiff but not dry, spread it over the top of the pudding, being sure to seal it to the edges. Bake in a preheated 350° oven about 15 minutes or until the meringue is brown. Serve at room temperature.

Another almost universal treat, bread pudding, is proof that if you waste not, you want not. In our household it was made with leftover biscuits. Bread pudding is one of those dishes that seems to accumulate variations. I've even heard of its being made with cornbread, but I tried it and didn't like the results. So what I'm giving you is the absolutely traditional way of making it. If you should stir some raisins or even some coconut into it, you may not find it half bad. In New Orleans, they make a lovely sauce using bourbon whiskey to pour on it. Neither of my grandmothers nor my Methodist mother would have approved of that, but you might want to check a good New Orleans cookbook for a recipe. You might even want to make the lemon sauce recipe which follows, using bourbon instead of the lemon juice. But don't blame me for enticing you into wickedness—I'm just reporting a *Louisiana* tradition.

Bread Pudding

leftover bread to fill a 1 quart dish loosely	2 cups milk
3 eggs	1 tablespoon vanilla
1 cup sugar	nutmeg

Break the bread into small pieces and place in an oven-proof dish. Beat together the sugar and the eggs and beat in the milk and add the vanilla. Pour the mixture over the bread and press the bread down into it. If there isn't enough liquid to come to the top of the bread, add more milk. Sprinkle the top with nutmeg. Allow to stand at least an hour. Bake in a 350° oven until puffed and brown, about 1 hour. Serve warm with cream or a sauce of your choice.

Rice pudding was done in exactly the same way, using cold leftover rice instead of the bread. I like it very much. I was an adult before I learned that rice was not to be cooked until it was just short of being gruel and then served with milk, butter, and sugar—it was another breakfast cereal so far as I was concerned. Because the modern trend is to cook rice much drier than in the old days, you have to be sure that rice pudding has plenty of liquid when it is baked. If you do, it will have a nice custard-like consistency. If you don't, it will be dry and unpalatable.

One of the great treats of all time—and one I wasn't deprived of—is ice cream. One of my very early memories is going with my mother and father to Sterchi's dairy in the Halls area to buy ice cream. I hope it was as good as I remember. If it was, I'm not sure why they are no longer there. In the spring, we even drove all the way over to Clinton Highway to Wallace's to get fresh peach ice cream.

We also made ice cream at home. To be willing to do it in those days, you really had to like ice cream. First, you had to go somewhere and buy a block of ice. This had to be chipped into pieces small enough to fit around the can in an old, crank-type ice cream churn. Second, a nice boiled custard had to be made and allowed to cool. (Before you ask—yes, we did sometimes make ice cream that was not cooked first. However, the several generations of women in my background would never admit that in public.) You then added additional milk and cream and some kind of flavoring (vanilla, fruit, berries, or whatever). This mixture was then placed in the can, the can placed in the churn, the ice and salt (I forgot to tell you about buying the salt, but you surely know we didn't mine it) and assign some man or some child to turn the crank until the mixture was frozen hard enough to make it difficult to turn. The paddle was then removed, the ice cream packed down, the hole plugged in the top of the can, more ice and salt added, and the whole thing wrapped in burlap bags for an hour or so. If it was not too late and everyone too tired, you then had ice cream. To go through all this, you had to like ice cream. We did.

A good old recipe is

Boiled Custard Ice Cream

4 eggs	1 quart of milk
1 cup sugar	1 pint of heavy cream
pinch of salt	flavoring

Beat the eggs with the sugar and salt. Add a little of the milk and beat until mixed. Add the rest of the milk and the cream and mix thoroughly. Cook over boiling water until thick. Stir in 1 tablespoon vanilla extract (or lemon extract, or a combination). Cool completely. Freeze in a 2-quart freezer, following the freezer directions.

Variations. If you prefer a fruit-flavored ice cream, simply leave out the vanilla or lemon and add pureed fresh fruit. Strawberries and peaches are both wonderful. Bananas are all right. Blueberries are interesting. Experiment a little to find which you like best.

I hesitate to tell you about one other form of ice cream because after telling you about it, I must caution you not to eat it. One of the terrible things that we have done to ourselves is to pollute the air to the point that snow ice cream is unsafe. Snow ice cream was just what the name implies, and it was heavenly. One of the things my wife and I disagree about (we never argue: we reason things out—sometimes you can hear us reasoning for blocks) is exactly how snow ice cream was made. She insists that you simply started with a bowl of snow and then beat in sugar, milk, and vanilla until it was the right consistency. I, on the other hand, know that you made boiled custard for ice cream, just as I described above, and then beat snow into the cooled custard until the right consistency was reached. If you were in a real hurry, you could simply beat sugar, milk, vanilla, and an egg together and then beat in the snow without cooking the mixture. However you made it, it was good. Now it is gone because snow isn't safe to eat. I miss it.

Cakes were also a regular part of the dessert scene. If you look at old pictures of special occasions, you will almost always see a cake. In a great many cases, it will be a coconut cake. I'm not sure why—I suppose that coconut represented the rare and exotic. For whatever reason, big cakes seemed to go with special events. But there were also everyday cakes, baked in a sheet pan and served hot with butter. Such a cake might be yellow or chocolate or perhaps even spice. All were good. A favorite sheet cake of mine was gingerbread. I found this recipe in an old book at my mother's, and she says she thinks it was one which Ma Freeman used. Whether it was or not, it makes a good snack or a fair dessert.

Old-Fashioned Gingerbread

5 tablespoons shortening	1 teaspoon ginger
½ cup sugar	1 teaspoon cinnamon
1 egg, well beaten	¼ teaspoon salt
½ cup molasses	1 teaspoon baking soda
1¾ cups flour	½ cup buttermilk

Cream the shortening and add the sugar. Beat in the egg. Add molasses and mix well. Sift together the flour and the spices. Mix the soda into the buttermilk. Add the dry ingredients and the milk alternately to the creamed mixture. Pour into a floured and greased 8-inch-square pan and bake in a preheated 350° oven about 45 minutes. Cut into squares and serve warm.

I particularly like spice cake. The following recipe will make two 8-inch layers (nice when iced with a caramel icing) or a 13-by-9-inch sheet. I prefer it the latter way, served warm with a lemon sauce.

Spice Cake

2½ cups sifted flour

1 cup sugar (you may use ½ cup white and ½ cup brown)

½ cup butter

1 teaspoon baking powder

1 teaspoon soda

½ teaspoon salt

1 teaspoon nutmeg

1 teaspoon allspice

¼ teaspoon cloves

2 eggs

1 cup buttermilk

Cream the butter and the sugar. Add the eggs one at a time, beating between. Sift together the flour, baking powder, soda, salt, and spices. Add the dry ingredients and the buttermilk alternately to the creamed mixture, beating well after each addition. Turn into greased and floured pans. Bake in a 350° oven until the cake is brown and the center is firm (about 30 minutes for layers and 40 to 45 minutes for a sheet cake.)

Note. If you don't have buttermilk on hand, use sweet milk. You will need to leave out the soda and add a comparable amount of baking powder.

Clear Lemon Sauce

2 tablespoons flour (or cornstarch)

1 cup sugar

2 cups cold water

2 egg yolks

½ cup fresh lemon juice (or 1 tablespoon lemon extract)

4 tablespoons butter

Mix together the flour and the sugar. Beat in the egg yolks. Stir in the cold water. Cook over medium heat, stirring constantly until the mixture boils and is thick. Remove from the heat and beat in the lemon and the butter. Serve hot.

Coconut cake may have been a festive dessert, but it wasn't hard to make. Often it was simply yellow cake layers iced with seven-minute frosting; coconut was put into the frosting between the layers and on the top and sides of the cake. (I assume you have your own favorite yellow layer cake. If not, just omit the spices from the spice cake above and you will have a nice yellow cake.) For really special occasions, you might have a white cake with coconut frosting. I haven't seen a white cake in years, maybe because they are not really worth the extra trouble. But here's a very old recipe that you might like to try.

White Cake

2¼ cups sifted flour

1½ cups sugar

½ teaspoon salt

2½ teaspoons baking powder

½ cup shortening (do not use butter)

4 egg whites

¾ cup milk

1 teaspoon vanilla

Cream together the sugar and the shortening. Add the egg whites and beat together. Sift the flour, salt, and baking powder together. Add alternately with the milk to the creamed mixture, beating well. (The old recipe really says to beat it 300 strokes.) Add the vanilla and stir it in. Pour into two 8-inch-diameter pans which have been greased and floured. Bake in a 350° oven for about 30 minutes or until lightly brown and the cake pulls free from the sides of the pan. Turn out to cool on a rack and when cool ice with seven-minute frosting. You may add coconut if you wish.

When I started writing this chapter, I thought everyone would have a recipe for seven-minute frosting right at hand, but in talking things over with friends, I found out that a lot of folks didn't even know what it was. So I'll give you a recipe.

Seven-Minute Frosting

1½ cups sugar

2 teaspoons light corn syrup

2 egg whites

5 tablespoons cold water

pinch of salt

pinch of cream of tartar

1 teaspoon vanilla

Combine the sugar, corn syrup, egg whites, water, salt, and cream of tartar in the top of a double boiler and place it over rapidly boiling water. Beat the mixture constantly with a rotary mixer (or portable electric mixer) while cooking. Continue beating and cooking until the frosting stands in peaks. Remove from the heat and stir in the vanilla.

This same frosting makes a nice **seafoam icing** if you use brown sugar instead of white. Although this frosting was traditionally done without the corn syrup, that is a very hit-and-miss proposition and I don't recommend it. I am told that without the corn syrup it works only on clear, cool days. Whatever! I still don't recommend it.

I've heard that it's practically illegal to publish a cookbook without including something chocolate, and I surely don't want to go against law or custom.

Devil's Food Cake

2 cups flour

½ cup cocoa

1½ cups sugar

1 teaspoon soda

¾ cup butter

2 eggs

½ cup buttermilk

½ cup hot water

1 teaspoon vanilla

Cream the butter with the sugar. Add the eggs and beat well. Sift together the dry ingredients. Add them alternately with the buttermilk. Stir in the hot water. Pour into two 8-inch layer pans or one 13-by-9-inch sheet pan, greased and floured. Bake in a preheated 350° oven until done. If you bake the cake as layers, allow them to cool and then frost with a chocolate fudge frosting. If you bake it as a sheet, you may frost the top or, preferably, serve hot with butter.

We also had pound cakes. Actually, I don't like the traditional pound cakes nearly so much as the more modern ones. I especially like pound cakes made with sour cream, and my friend Betty Castellaw makes a pound cake with powdered sugar which is heavenly. But unfortunately it is not traditional—and you know what a purist I am—so it will just have to wait till my next book.

I have, however, saved to the end two cakes which are so much a part of East Tennessee tradition that it would be unthinkable to omit them from a book on the cooking of this area in my lifetime. The first of these is blackberry jam cake. Back in "Summer" I told you about my personal antipathy to blackberries. But however great it is, I don't let it stop me from enjoying this wonderfully moist, rich cake. This recipe is my mother's, and getting it written down was not an easy task. My mother, like her mother before her, cooks by putting some ingredients into a bowl and stirring them up. She measures little. She knows how much she needs and she puts it in. I have arrived at the jam cake recipe by watching her make it. I have tried the recipe and it works. I can't convince myself that it's quite so good as hers, but I guess that can't be avoided.

Blackberry Jam Cake

1 cup sugar	¼ teaspoon cloves
½ cup shortening	1 teaspoon soda
2 eggs	2 teaspoons baking powder
2 cups flour	½ teaspoon salt
1 teaspoon cinnamon	1 cup buttermilk
½ teaspoon allspice	1 cup blackberry jam
½ teaspoon nutmeg	1 cup raisins, lightly floured

Cream together the shortening and the sugar. Add the eggs. Sift together the flour, spices, soda, baking powder, and salt. Add alternately to the creamed mixture with the buttermilk. Fold in the jam and the raisins.

Pour into 2 greased and floured 9-inch-diameter pans and bake at 350° about 25 to 30 minutes or until done. Cool on a rack and frost with caramel frosting.

I am going to give you two caramel frostings which I like. The first is the traditional way of making it with cream, sugar, and butter. When it works, it is very good. Unfortunately, if you don't cook it exactly right, it either spends the afternoon running off the cake or resembles cream-colored marble. The second variation is newer but is very forgiving if you are not too exact. This way you can know what we used to do and still have a great cake every time.

Traditional Caramel Icing

1 cup sugar

1 cup brown sugar (firmly packed)

⅔ cup sweet cream

1 teaspoon vanilla

Combine the sugars and the cream in a heavy saucepan and cook over medium heat to the soft ball stage (234°). Remove from the heat and cool to lukewarm. Add the vanilla and beat to spreading consistency. If the icing becomes too firm, too soon, add cream to soften.

Dependable Caramel Icing

½ cup butter, melted

1 cup brown sugar (firmly packed)

¼ cup milk

¼ teaspoon salt

1 teaspoon vanilla

2 cups powdered sugar, sifted

Combine the butter and brown sugar over low heat until the sugar is dissolved. Add the milk and return to the heat and allow to come to a boil. Remove from the heat and allow to cool to lukewarm. Add the vanilla and the powdered sugar and beat to spreading consistency. You may add more powdered sugar if the icing is too soft or more milk if it is too firm.

Now, at last, we arrive at what I still consider to be the best of all East Tennessee desserts. Apple stack cake is almost universal in this area. The only thing more universal than the cake itself is the disagreement over how it is to be made and how it is to be stacked. I'm going to give you the version I like, and then I'll tell you about some of the possible variations.

Apple Stack Cake

The cake:

4 cups flour	½ cup buttermilk
¼ teaspoon salt	1 cup sugar
½ teaspoon soda	1 egg
1 teaspoon baking powder	1½ teaspoons vanilla
½ cup shortening	1½ teaspoons lemon extract

Cream together the shortening and the sugar. Add the egg. Add the salt, soda, baking powder, the buttermilk, and 2 cups of the flour. Beat until well blended. Continue to beat and work in the extra flour. (I do this with the dough hook on the Kitchenaid mixer. It is a tough job by hand.) The dough should be fairly firm and still sticky. Turn out on a heavily floured surface and knead in additional flour until the dough is smooth, firm, and no longer sticky. Divide the dough into six even portions. Roll each portion to fit a 9-inch-diameter cake pan, which you have greased and floured. Press the dough firmly into the pan, being sure it is in the pan evenly and goes up to the edge of the pan. Bake in a 350° oven until brown (about 15 minutes). Repeat until all the layers have been baked.

The apples:

3 cups home-dried apple slices	½ cup sugar (approximately)
5 cups water (approximately)	½ teaspoon cinnamon

Wash the apples and place them in a pan with a tight-fitting lid with the water. Cover, bring to a boil, and reduce the heat until the apples barely simmer. Cook until the apples are very soft and mash easily. If all the water is absorbed, add more water. If the apples are not very thick, cook uncovered until they are thick. Sweeten to taste and add the cinnamon. Mash the apples completely.

The assembly:

When the cake is completely cool and the apples just warm, place a cake layer on a double thickness of foil or on a plate that will fit into a metal box with a tight-fitting lid. Spread ⅕ of the apples on the cake, being sure to spread them to the very edges of the cake layer. Repeat with cake layers and apples, using ⅕ of the apples each time. End with your best-looking cake layer. Wrap the cake completely in the foil or place in an airtight box and allow to stand 24 hours before serving.

You may want to modify the above instructions slightly. Five layers make a nice cake. I'd suggest taking the dough for that sixth layer and making it into **tea cakes**. These large cookies were generally made fairly thick and served with apples to spread on them. They are also good made very thin and crisp. In either case, you roll the dough as thick as you would like it and cut it into cookies. Transfer each cookie to a lightly greased cookie sheet, brush it with water, and sprinkle it with granulated sugar. Bake until lightly browned. If you decide on this option, simply increase the amount of apples slightly between each layer of the cake or keep it about as it was and have the rest to eat with the cookies.

My mother's family sometimes made **spiced cake layers**. If you wish to try this variation, use ½ cup sugar and ½ cup molasses. Add about ½ teaspoon cinnamon, ½ teaspoon nutmeg, and about ⅛ teaspoon of ginger and cloves to the cake mixture and proceed as above. You may need just a little more flour— remember, keep kneading in flour until the dough is *very* stiff. Prepare the apples just as we did above.

This spicy version of the cake dough was the basis of one of the delights of children, at least in our household. By reducing the amount of the other spices to ¼ teaspoon each and increasing the amount of ginger to ½ teaspoon, you get a wonderful, pliant dough for making **gingerbread men**. Heads, bodies, arms, and legs were each shaped separately and pressed together on a cookie sheet. They were then finished with raisins for eyes, nose, mouth and buttons. (Yes, buttons. You don't think we would have let that gingerbread child run around naked, do you?) When they read to me about the little gingerbread man who ran away and got into all kinds of trouble, I knew exactly what he looked like.

In modern times, people have claimed that you can make all kinds of substitutions for the fairly hard-to-find home-dried apples to make stack cakes. They are right—you can. The cakes just aren't as good. I know people who use applesauce, apple butter, and a mixture of the two. I have even known people who used strawberry preserves. You may like one or more of these. I absolutely do not recommend using commercially dried apples. As I pointed out earlier, they are treated to keep them white and it completely changes the taste and the texture.

If you are to enjoy this treat, I recommend drying your own apples. If, however, this seems too much trouble and you are fortunate enough to be in the East Tennessee area, I am happy to tell you that the Apple Barn between Sevierville and Pigeon Forge now has good untreated dried apples. When you are in that area, stop at this delightful store located in an apple orchard. They have a nice restaurant there as well, where you can get a whole range of well-prepared apple dishes—sometimes even stack cake.

For ending a book on the food of East Tennessee, it would be difficult to find anything more appropriate than apple stack cake. I have ended a lot of good meals with them. God willing, I will end many more. And whenever I reach the end of such a meal and taste the sweet, soft taste of custard pie, or coconut cream pie, or apple stack cake, I will remember people who are gone. I will remember Granny and Grandpa Weaver, who managed to raise six children on a small East Tennessee farm. I will remember gruff old Grandpa reading to me while we sat on the front porch swing or taking me to the Popeye Club at the Tennessee Theater while he did his shopping downtown. I will remember Dad Dossett saying "A, apple pie . . ." and Mammy hiding a custard pie. I will remember my mother teaching me how to cook, partly out of necessity and partly because she thought everyone should know. Memories of food call forth memories of people I shared it with.

And now let's end on that note. There's as much that I haven't included as there is that I have. But I hope that this little book will cause you to examine for yourself the role food plays in your life. Consider those times when someone who is trying to reach out has chosen food as the way to do it—those times when a loaf of bread or an apple pie is a way of saying you care that goes beyond words.

Think, too, of your heritage. Whether you are from East Tennessee or Eastern China, there are distinctive parts of your experience and especially of the foods that are part of it which should not be lost. Write them down. Teach them to your children. Tell your friends about them. Tell me about it. While you're doing it, come sit down and have a piece of cake and a cup of coffee. The cake is still warm and I have some nice sweet butter . . .

Index

Fresh Cucumbers in Vinegar, 61
Fried
    Apple Pies, 98
    Apples, 35
    Cabbage, 67
    Chicken, Traditional, 77, 80
        Variations, 81
    Corn, 36, 48
    Cornbread, 170
    Country Ham, 141
    Green Tomatoes, 59
    Mush, 108
    Okra, 51
Frosting, Seven-Minute, 193
Fruit-Flavored Ice Cream, 189
Fruit Pie, 40, 177

Gingerbread,
    Old-Fashioned, 190
Gingerbread Men, 198
Goldenrod Eggs, 33
Grape
    Cobbler, 88
        Variation, 88
    Juice, 88
    Pie, 88
    Preserves, 88
Grapes
    Concord, 87, 88
    Muscadines, 87
    Scuppernong, 87
Grapevines, 87
Gravy
    Beef, 125
    Milk, 81, 82
    Red-Eye, 142
    Tomato, 113
Green
    Beans, 54
        Dried, 55

Green, continued
    Onions, 29, 30
    Peas, 26
    Tomato
        Fried, 59
        Lime Pickles, 60
        "Mangoes" (Pickles), 70
        Pie, 61
Greens, 25, 109
    Boiling Method, 110
    Collards, 109
    Curly Mustard, 109
    Kale, 109
    Parboiling Method, 110
    Poke Salat, 23–25
    Pokeweed, 23–25
    Turnip, 109
    Wild, 23
Grimes Golden (Apples), 87
Grits, Hominy, 107

Hach, Phila Rawlings, 50, 170
Ham, 34
    Country, Baked, 144
    Fried, 141
    Half-Cured, 152
Hard-Cooked Eggs, 32
Hay, 45
Hog
    Curing, 131
    Jowl, with Black-Eyed Peas, 155
    Killing, 129, 131
Hollyhocks, 30
Home-Fried Potatoes, 151
Homemade Light Bread, 160
Hominy, 107
    Grits, 107
Honey, Pear, 99
"Horse Pears," 87, 99
Hot Cakes, 36